Five
Simple
Steps

the

HANDBOOK

BY **JON HICKS** · FOREWORD BY **THE NOUN PROJECT**

The Icon Handbook
by Jon Hicks

Published in 2011 by Five Simple Steps
Studio Two, The Coach House
Stanwell Road
Penarth
CF64 3EU
United Kingdom

On the web: *www.fivesimplesteps.com*
Please send errors to *errata@fivesimplesteps.com*

Publisher: Five Simple Steps
Editor: Chris Mills
Tech Editors: Gedeon Maheux, Andy Clarke
Copy Editor: Owen Gregory
Production Manager: Sarah Morris
Design & Art Direction: Nick Boulton, Colin Kersley, Jon Hicks, Mark Boulton, Nathan Ford, Alex Morris
Front Cover Illustration: Jon Hicks

ISBN: 978-1-907828-03-4

A catalogue record of this book is available from the British Library.

For Leigh, Daniel and Samantha, who said "I'd buy the book, even though it'll be boring..."

Acknowledgements

Without these people this book wouldn't exist, so in Oscar acceptance speech style, thanks must go out to:

Leigh, for putting up with me while writing the book, and being encouraging without fail. I can't have been easy to live with.

My mum and dad, for giving me the opportunities I needed to get where I am now.

Emma, Nick and Mark Boulton, Colin Kersley, Sarah Morris and everyone else at Mark Boulton Design and Five Simple Steps for taking the project on and making it real.

My mentor and guru throughout the whole project, Chris Mills, for encouragement, inspiration and laughs.

My words team: Owen Gregory, Gedeon Maheux, Andy Clarke and the Noun Project, for getting on board so enthusiastically.

Opera Software, and Knut, Oleg and Tami in particular, for being so flexible and understanding when I had to down tools for a day to work on "the damn book". You really are great clients to work with. My friends and fellow office sharers Simon Clayson, Jon Dennis and Matt Hamm, for being there to bounce ideas and get invaluable gut reactions.

All the wonderful contributors and helpers, particularly for responding so quickly and so enthusiastically:

AIGA; Brian Amerige (*Five Details*); Gerd Arntz web archive (*www.gerdarntz.org*); Wolfgang Bartelme (*Bartelme Design*); Martin Beeby (*Microsoft UK*); Diane Bilbey (*Department of Typography & Graphic Communication, University of Reading*);

Tobias Bjerrome Ahlin (*Spotify*); Doug Bowman (*Twitter*); Dan Cederholm (*Dribbble.com*); Sebastiaan de With (*Double Twist*); Nik Fletcher (*Realmac Software*); Jasper Hauser (*Sofa*); Jono Hunt (*Iconaholic*); Mark Jardine (*Tapbots*); Susan Kare; Tariq Krim (*Jolicloud*); David Lanham (*The Iconfactory*); Fred le Blanc (*FredHQ*); Lucian Marin; Mischa McLachlan; Mark McLaughlin (*Skype*); Jeff McMorris (*CodeGoo*); Susie Mulhern, PARC; Pieter Omvlee (*Bohemian Coding*); Sergey Perets (*Artua*); Jeff Rock (*Mobelux*); Cabel Sasser (*Panic Software*); Paul Sladen (*Canonical*); Kyle Tezak; Jan Van Boghout (*MacRabbit*); Aaron Walter and Ben Chestnut (*Mailchimp*); Josh Williams (*Gowalla*); Drew Wilson.

Finally to Andy Sellick, for always appearing genuinely interested whenever he asked me how the book was going. Well, I'm finished! Can we go for a ride now, please?

Image credits

The majority of the icons in the cover design are my own, but it also features artwork from the following sources:

Public domain icons from the Noun Project (*http://thenounproject.com*) as well as: bicycle, cheese, angel, wine and tree.
The Glyphish icon set *http://glyphish.com/*

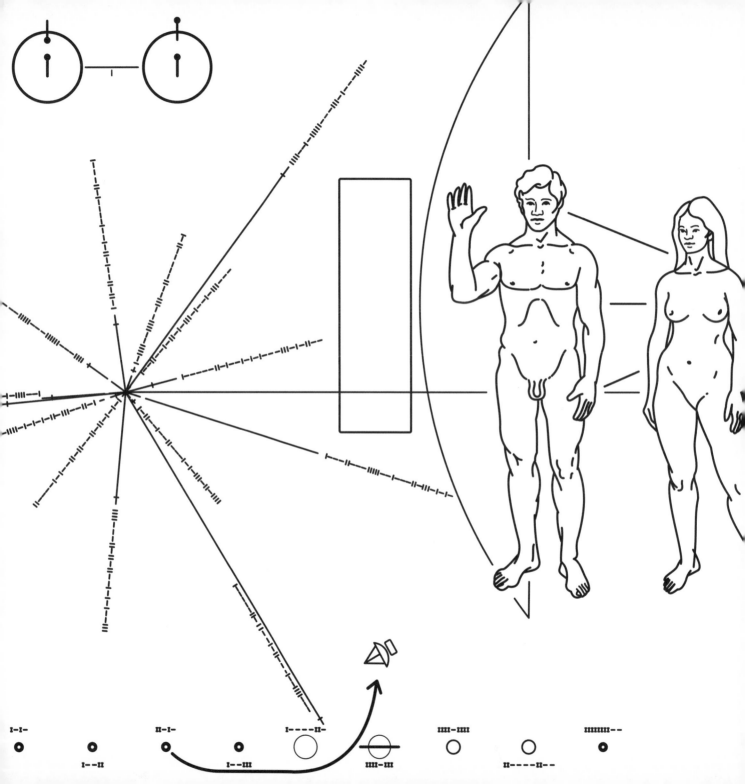

Foreword

Approximately nine and a half billion miles from Earth, the American space satellite Pioneer 10 continues its lonely journey through the outer reaches of our solar system. If the space probe is ever discovered by another intelligent life form, the extraterrestrials will find a gold-plated plaque affixed to the side of the satellite. Engraved on this plaque is a pictorial message that communicates the essence of our human species and the location of planet Earth.

I can think of no greater example than the Pioneer plaque to demonstrate the universal communicative power of symbols. Imagine all the sophisticated technology embedded in this satellite. Yet, when tasked with telling the most important story, the story of the human race, scientists relied on hieroglyphs, one of the most basic and ancient forms of communication. They did this because they knew symbols have the power to transcend any cultural or even cosmic barrier and deliver information effortlessly and effectively.

It comes as no surprise then, that in our ever shrinking and highly technological world, symbols, because of their universal communicative power, have become the preferred language of the internet age. In the past few years alone there has been an explosion of new symbols and icons added to the lexicon, and this trend shows no signs of stopping. Think of all the symbols that have been created to represent concepts around social media: tweet; like; share; link; blog; user. These symbols have become and will remain a part of our everyday life. Now imagine all the symbols that will be needed to represent new concepts in medicine, nanotechnology, environmental protection, human rights and augmented reality. It is safe to say designers are poised to exponentially expand the world's visual language vocabulary over the coming years, and this book will be an invaluable tool to assist them.

Edward J Boatman
Co-founder of the Noun Project

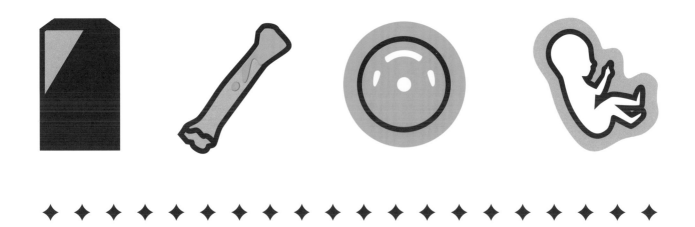

2001: A SPACE ODYSSEY

"Trying to capture the essence of an object or idea with only a few lines and at the same time maintaining its elegance is pretty much design in a nutshell. That's what's so great about icons, they're tiny poems."

Kyle Tezak, The Four Icon Challenge

Introduction

I was brought up — as I'm sure you were — with icons all around me, especially in the home. The stereo and TV had them, the labels in my clothes had them, and so did the machine that washed them. Whenever we travelled in the car, I would record the road signs I saw in my iSpy book, and see what landmarks were near us on an Ordnance Survey map with the aid of the key. The difference between 'Church with Tower' and 'Church with Spire' is forever etched into my consciousness.

Broadcasting station (mast or tower)

Bus or coach station

Church with tower

with spire

without tower or spire

or Chapel

Glasshouse

Graticule intersection at 5' intervals

...icity transmission line
...h pylons spaced conventionally)

...pe line
(arrow indicates direction of flow)

Quarry

Open pit

Wood

Orchard

...rk or ornamental gr...

I-SPY

15p

STAR...
BOO...

My father was a keen meteorologist, so the first time I was particularly aware of icons was through the daily routine of BBC weather reports. Michael Fish would slap them on to the map, where they would stick 90% of the time.

Icons are little miracle workers. They circumvent language obstacles, give concise warnings and directions, convey our moods and show which buttons to press. Anyone needing to find a toilet in an unfamiliar country has been thankful for the familiar sign that not only shows where it is, but which one to use. The rise of desktop computers, and better and better mobile devices has extended icon use even further, with an abundance of applications requiring icons to differentiate between them and navigate their interfaces.

To some, however, icons are little more than a decorative flourish, merely a means of making a text-heavy design look more appealing. Either the designer misunderstands their advantages, or overuses them, creating a Christmas tree effect, confusing the eye and distracting the visitor.

This is a book that I've been wanting to write for a long time. Whenever I've looked for a book on this subject, the only available publications are reference guides that simply reproduce as many symbols as possible. Where books have gone into theory, they were published decades before desktop computers, and therefore miss the most relevant and active context of icon use. Sometimes the topic is covered as a part of a book about logo design, and amounts to little more than a page or two. So I've set out to create the manual, reference guide and coffee table book that I always desired.

It's aimed at designers who already have basic vector and bitmap drawing skills. It could be that you only have to create a simple favicon, or perhaps you've been asked to work on a website or mobile app that requires icons. You might usually rely on a resource like a royalty-free icon set, which may provide common icons but probably doesn't provide everything you need.

This book begins at the point when you need to create your own icons. Its purpose is to guide relatively inexperienced designers through an icon design workflow, starting with favicons and working up to application icons, as well as inspiring and providing a reference point for existing icon designers. It does not set out to teach you how to draw in a particular application, although it does highlight the pitfalls of particular graphic editors and explain their individual advantages. The aim is not to improve proficiency in particular applications but, rather, to show you how to create icons with the common toolset found in most of them, so you can be more versatile.

Before we go any further though, there's something we need to clear up...

What is an icon?

Leaving aside the religious connotations of the term, the word 'icon' today covers a wide range of image types, from monochrome play and pause buttons to the highly detailed, full-colour icons used to identify an application. They can be as simple as a triangle, or as complex as a photorealistic leaf with veins and droplets of water, but they all live under the broad umbrella of icons.

One distinction we need to draw early on is that between an icon and a logo. Logos are unique identifiers that work best when they stand out among other logos. Icons, on the other hand, generally don't communicate a corporate identity; rather, they inform, translate and warn. They tell us which route to take, which buttons to press and what danger is ahead; they work best when they're familiar and recognisable. Finding a toilet in a foreign airport would be so much harder if the sign used the Armitage Shanks logo instead of the familiar man and woman symbols.

Throughout this book, I will refer to icons as being '32px' or '128px'. Icons are measured in pixels (px) and nearly always squared (there are only a couple of exceptions) so these examples would refer to 'a 32-pixel squared icon' or 'a 128×128-pixel squared icon'. Where the dimensions aren't squared, such as the iPhone4's document icons, these will be written as '44×58px'. And although icons for Apple's Retina display require their areas to be squared, to avoid confusion I'll stick to established convention and say they're twice the size, since their dimensions are doubled.

The structure of this book intends to take you through the creation of various different types of icons, building up the skills as we go.

Favicons

Unlike other icons, favicons will almost always be a smaller version of a website logo. Originally used in a browser's address bar and bookmarks views, they're now used in a much wider variety of contexts. Their simplicity makes them a great starting point for our journey.

Favicons are covered in chapter 3.

Ideograms, pictograms and arbitrary icons

The kind of icons used in websites and user interfaces are often either a picture of something (pictograms), an idea of something (ideograms) or an invention (arbitrary). Often just monochrome, these icons help us find our way and make actions and functions clearer.

We'll look at them in chapter 5.

Application icons

Mostly photorealistic, these blur the distinction between logos and icons, sitting somewhere in between. With the ever-growing production rate of apps, the variety of popular devices and platforms these apps are consumed on and the increasing resolutions that need to be created now, this type of icon is important. Application icons are discussed in chapter 7.

   Before we go too deep into the detail of the various types, their uses and how to draw them, it would be best to start with the story of icons and understand how we got here.

References

http://kyletezak.com/portfolio/the-four-icon-challenge/

Table
of
Contents

Chapter 1

A potted history of icons

Let's start the journey from the very beginning and look at the development of a symbolic language to complement our written one, how previous works have influenced modern icon design, and how the meaning of icons has evolved from religious art to encompass software. As part of the journey, I'll also delve into how I became involved with designing icons as early as 1984.

A potted history of icons

Long before cultures developed any form of written language, as far back as 100,000 years ago, humans have communicated using symbols and pictures. These images — painted on to cave walls (pictographs) or carved into rock (petroglyphs) — were not only art. They were made to record events and tell stories about food and shelter, using symbols to convey repeated themes. The simplest icon of all, the circle, was used to represent the sun but developed over time to be more abstract, conveying concepts of heat and light instead.

While the first sun symbol is a pictogram (a picture of a thing), later versions are known as ideograms because they convey the idea of heat or light, a more abstract concept. A similar kind of representative imagery shows up later (5,000 years ago) in other places such as Chinese writing and, in particular, ancient Egyptian hieroglyphics. The hieroglyphic for house is based on a floor plan, while the glyph for water is even more obvious.

For many cultures this has been the case until fairly recently. In Britain, there is no surviving evidence of any written language until the Romans brought us Latin just 2,000 years ago.

In addition to pictograms representing an object and ideograms conveying an abstract idea or concept, there is a third type of icon. In his *Symbol Sourcebook*, Henry Dreyfuss describes this kind as 'arbitrary'. These are symbols that have been invented but do not relate to a physical object: their meaning has to be learned rather than deduced. When German mathematician Johannes Widmann published his book of arithmetic in 1489, it was the first time we ever saw the + (plus) and - (minus) signs in print. Their meaning could not be determined by examination alone: we only understand them because we have acquired that knowledge.

Egyptian hieroglyphs for house and water

Nothing here

 Owner is in

 Owner is out

 Best place for handout

 Police here don't like hobos

 OK/Alright

 This is not a safe place

 Kind lady lives here

 Dangerous drinking water

 Dangerous neighbourhood

This is the place

Hobo signs

In the same way, during the Great Plague of England in 1665–66, the front doors of infected houses were painted with a large red cross by plague doctors to warn others away. We still use a red X as a warning sign today.

From the 1880s until the 1940s, hobos who rode the rails across the United States would leave cryptic symbols on fences, footpaths, street signs and railway stops to help other hobos find their way. These would provide vital information such as where they could rest or eat, how hospitable the locals were, local law enforcement status and the best approaches for a handout. Whenever a hobo arrived in a new town, they would seek out these signs first to see if a stopover would even be worth the risk. In a sense, they were reviving the spirit of the early cave painters.

Isotype

Up to this point, icons were generally still localised efforts, which communicated information within a culture, and not necessarily outside of it. That changed with the groundbreaking work of Viennese philosopher Otto Neurath in the early 1920s and 1930s. Influenced by his love of Egyptian hieroglyphics, Neurath believed that the world needed a unified, international visual language to support (but not replace) each of the world's spoken languages. Known as Isotype (International System of Typographic Picture Education), he and his team of artists headed by Gerd Arntz developed a system of pictograms, which could be combined with other standard elements such as a triangle with red border, to add more meaning and variations.

When Neurath died suddenly at the end of 1945, his work was carried on by his wife Marie, and is now archived at the University of Reading. Their work wouldn't look at all out of place in graphic design today, and you can clearly see the origins of modern infographics and road signage in his creations.

5

Isotype linocut and print, Gerd Arntz, 1930s
Archive Gemeentemuseum,
The Hague, The Netherlands
Photo: Max Bruinsma

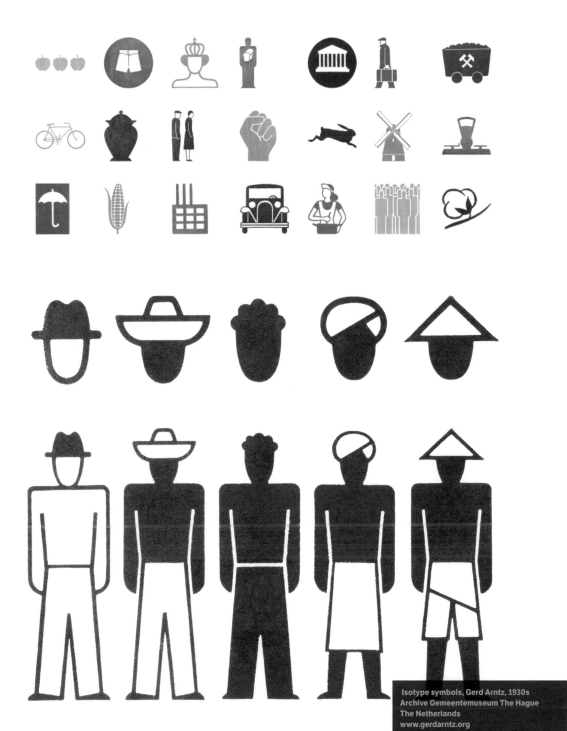

Isotype symbols, Gerd Arntz, 1930s
Archive Gemeentemuseum The Hague
The Netherlands
www.gerdarntz.org

572 232 572 404 86 825,1120 801 154 823 803 7054/K 97 917 243

1045

1626

1633

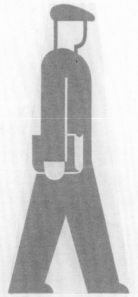

1085

1061

1037

SYMBOLS OF PICTORIAL STATISTICS

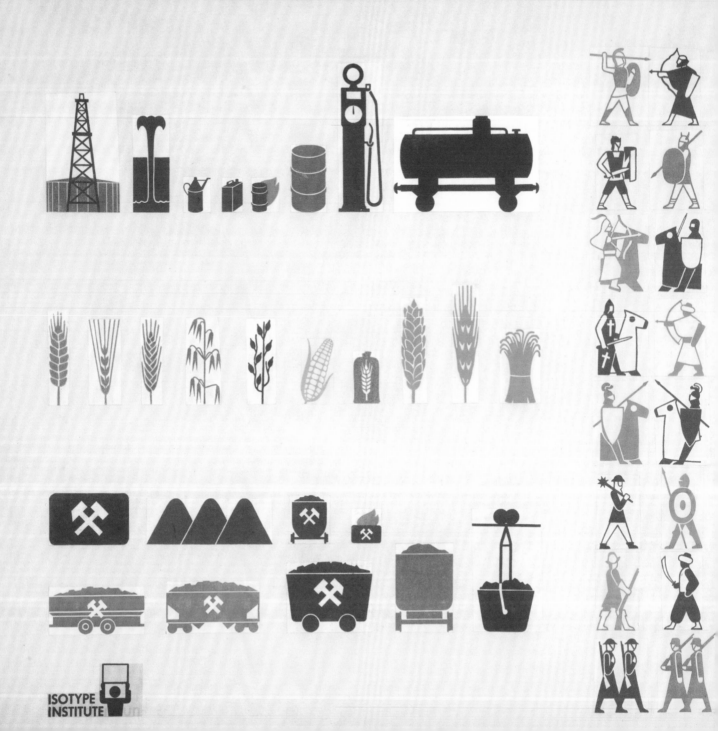

ISOTYPE INSTITUTE

Symbols of Pictorial Statistics chart.
Otto and Marie Neurath Isotype Collection
University of Reading

Gerd Arntz can be credited with being the originator of the pictogram style we still use today. In particular, the influence of Neurath's Isotype work can be seen two decades later, in the pictograms designed to represent individual sports for each of the Olympic Games from 1964 to 1972. The team created a clean geometric identity for the Games, which itself is a design classic, and the pictograms typify the cool, precise and logical approach they took. No line is wasted in these symbols: everything is pared down to its absolute minimum.

Symbols from the 1972 (left), 1968 (right) and 1964 (far right) Olympic Games

Symbols from the 1964 Olympic Games

However, when we think of icons, we probably most commonly think of their use on computers. The first computer icons appeared as early as 1974 on the Xerox Alto, a machine named after the Palo Alto Research Center (PARC) where it was developed. While much of its interface was still text-based, it had a mouse (and therefore a pointer) and a painting package containing the familiar icon-based tools window that we still use today.

It was a research tool intended for organisations like universities, and wasn't available to purchase by the public. It was no less influential despite this, inspiring the Xerox Star Workstation that followed it in 1981, and the first personal computer with a graphical user interface — the Apple Lisa — in 1983.

It was after the creation of the Alto that the term icon was coined in a PhD thesis by David Canfield Smith, a computer science graduate student at Stanford University in California. Alan Kay from the Alto team at PARC suggested that he look at using the graphics possibilities of the Alto to help people program.

> *"Smith reused the term from the Russian Orthodox church, where an icon is more than an image, because it embodies properties of what it represents: a Russian icon of a saint is holy and is to be venerated. Smith's computer icons contained all the properties of the programs and data represented, and therefore could be linked or acted on as if they were the real thing."*
> **Spectrum, September 1989, pp. 46–51.**

The word itself comes from Greek εἰκών (eikōn), which has two meanings: likeness or image, both of which apply to icons.

While much of the Alto's UI was still text-based, the Star used icons much more widely. It was the first computer to have a GUI and it also started the now familiar office metaphor of desktop, files, folders and wastebaskets that we still use today. Norm Cox was responsible for designing the icon set, and it's here that we have the first appearance of the document icon with folded top-right corner. His style used rounded rectangles with distinctive heavy strokes to give contrast.

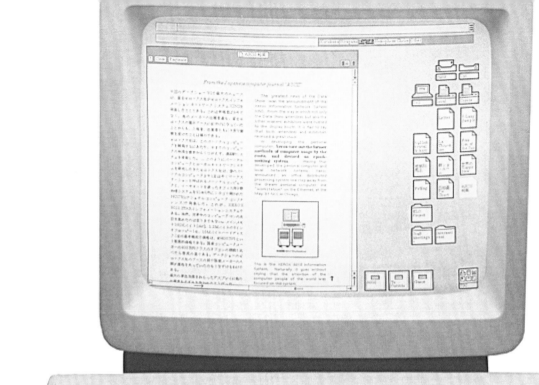

The Xerox 8010 (aka, Star) Workstation. © PARC, a Xerox company

Working with 1-bit depth (either black or white pixels), Cox found ways to make the best of those bitmap limitations. By making background patterns stepped, the effect of ragged edges on the icons could be eliminated.

> *"Many users, for example, said they lost time having to read through the lists of commands shown on the screen, so Xerox has substituted "icons" — or command symbols. If you want Star to file something, roll the mouse and move the cursor to a picture of an appropriately labeled file folder; for storing deleted material, point to the picture of a wastebasket."*
>
> **'Xerox xooms towards the office of the future', Fortune, 18 May 1981, pp. 44–52**

How I started

Many icon designers trace the beginnings of their interest back to making sprites for video games and I'm no different. Back in 1984 our family got an Acorn Electron, a home computer based on the BBC Micro, with the added benefit of being a bit cheaper! Laughable now, but connecting it to the TV was magical: one of those moments when you feel like the future has finally arrived.

My first experience of coding was with BBC Basic, creating 8×8 pixel sprites for simple games like Bugzap. As my coding skills didn't really get much further than:
10 PRINT "HELLO",20 "GOTO10", I relied on magazines that would print the code for simple games, which I would then slavishly retype. This provided the opportunity to replace the sprites with my own designs, so that a simple driving game could become an X-Wing doing a trench run, for example.

The first stage was to draw the artwork in the 8×8 grid supplied in the back of the Electron manual (in pencil, of course — this would get erased and reused many times). This was then converted into a VDU code by adding up the values of the columns in each row, as seen at the top of the next page.

When I left school to study illustration and design at art college towards the end of the 1980s, I had my first experience of using a computer with a GUI: in this case, the Mac. The college was kitted out with now legendary Mac Classics, and I became aware of the groundbreaking icon work Susan Kare had done for Mac System Software 1.0.

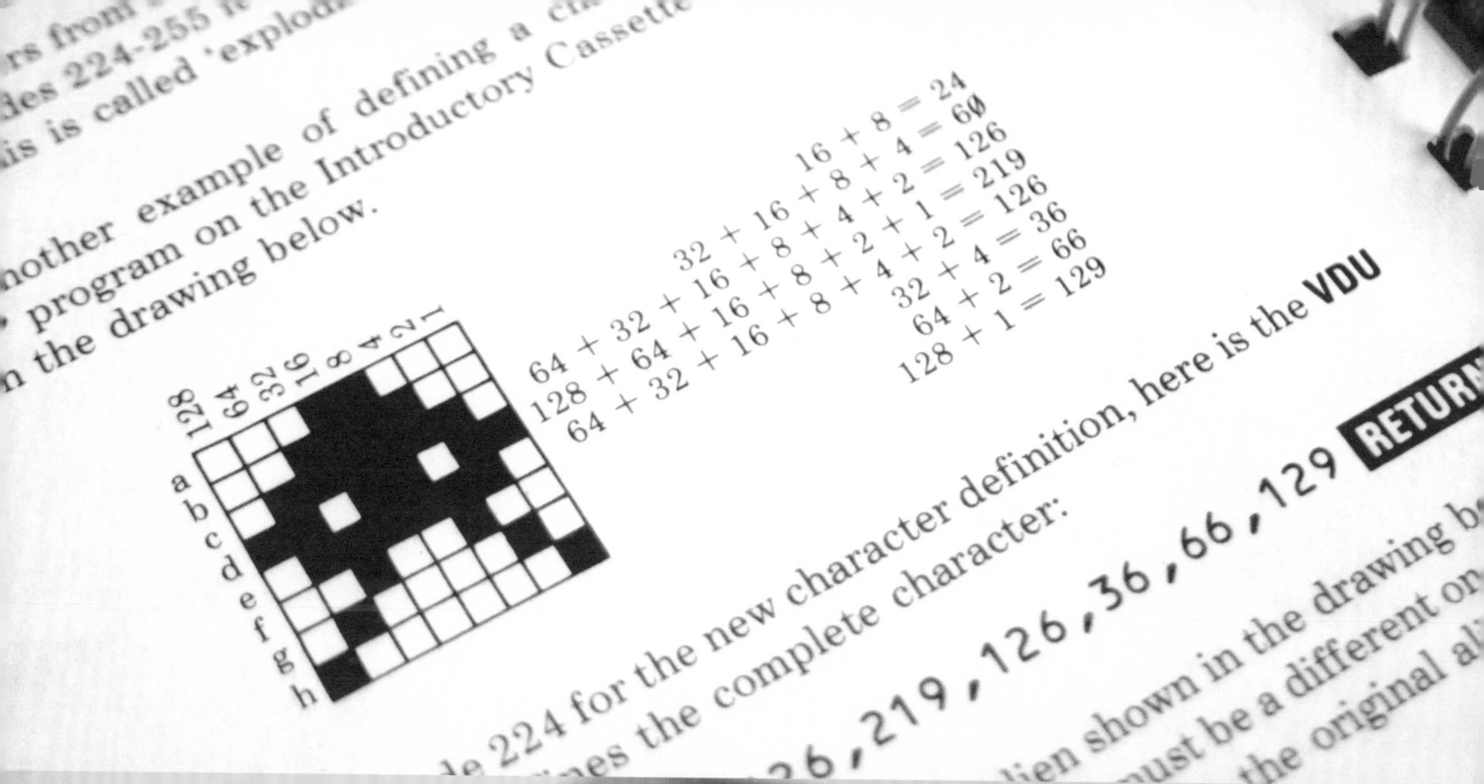

rs from
des 224-255 i
is is called 'explod

nother example of defining a ch
program on the Introductory Cassette
n the drawing below.

$$16 + 8 = 24$$
$$16 + 8 + 4 = 60$$
$$32 + 16 + 8 + 4 + 2 = 126$$
$$64 + 32 + 16 + 8 + 4 + 2 + 1 = 219$$
$$128 + 64 + 16 + 8 + 2 + 1 = 126$$
$$64 + 32 + 16 + 8 + 4 + 2 = 126$$
$$32 + 4 = 36$$
$$64 + 2 = 66$$
$$128 + 1 = 129$$

de 224 for the new character definition, here is the **VDU**

pes the complete character:

6,219,126,36,66,129 **RETURN**

ien shown in the drawing b
ust be a different on
the original ali

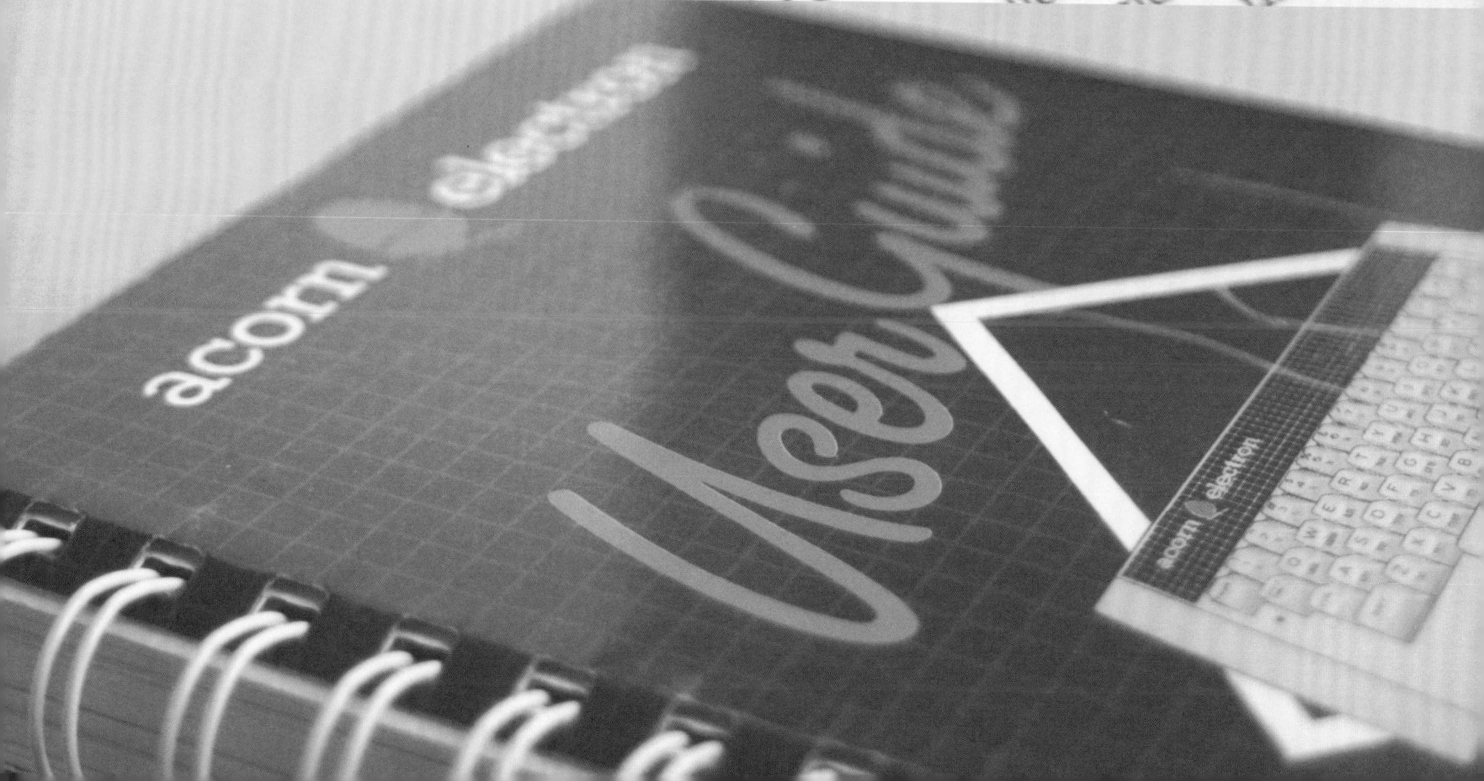

Susan Kare's original icons for the Macintosh System Software 1.0

Quite simply, when I think of icons I think of Susan Kare. Hailed by the Museum of Modern Art in New York as "a pioneering and influential computer iconographer" she developed the original icons for Macintosh System Software 1.0. Everything I know and love about icons is embodied in that work from 1984, and it took until 2001 before the Mac OS icons progressed to any significant degree. Her famous animated wristwatch icon to let the user know a task is in progress is still used today in Adobe Photoshop. I was lucky enough to get the chance to interview Susan for this book.

First of all, many thanks for agreeing to be a part of The Icon Handbook. I particularly wanted to feature the original Mac icons as they encapsulate everything that icons should be and are, of course, design classics.

You're known for the original Mac icons but I've heard that your background up to that point was in sculpture. How did the project with Apple come about?

" I had the opportunity to join the Macintosh project thanks to my high school friend, Andy Hertzfeld, who was a software lead. He needed some bitmaps so encouraged me to develop some early images on graph paper.

As it was such a new discipline at that point, was there any previous skill or experience that helped you? Was the lack of previous work in that area a help or a hindrance?

I had a fair amount of experience in traditional graphic design so was able to build on that, plus common sense. Yes, a new medium but in another sense there is nothing new under the sun. I joke that if you can do needlepoint, you can design bitmap graphics.

What tools did you use to design the original Mac icons other than sketching? Did you have a graphical editor to work with?

Andy Hertzfeld wrote a bitmap editor for me that displayed the icon grid at 100% and enlarged so I could see how everything looked. It also automatically generated the hex equivalent. Not too many tools initially, but it worked really well.

You also designed the Apple Command icon that is now an accepted convention. How did you come up with a symbol for such an abstract concept?

I leafed through a book of symbols, and came across a similar cloverleaf, which was identified as an image used on signs in Swedish campgrounds to mean 'interesting feature'. This seemed appropriate, and would lend itself to being re-created in a limited number of pixels, plus fit well on a squarish key cap. Years later, I learned that it is meant to be a castle, seen from above.

Finally, what do you find are the differences (if any) designing icons now compared to the original Mac icons?

Obviously, more pixels and more colours affords a greater range of stylistic options but, conceptually, the design problem is similar — what image can you create in a limited piece of screen real estate to communicate a particular idea at a glance? It was a terrific opportunity to work on the original Macintosh with so many talented colleagues.

Continuing my journey

When Mac OS 8 arrived in 1997, I started drawing icons again, using ResEdit to play around with the system icons. I was no longer limited to an 8×8 pixel size with limited colour palette: 32 pixels allowed so much more space for artwork, and with a wider range of colours.

My interest up to this point was still restricted to merely fiddling around for a bit of fun, but when I went freelance in 2002 and bought my first Mac with OS X 10.1, my interest in icon design began in earnest. Icons could now be as large as 128 pixels, allowing for a much greater level of detail, as part of a much richer UI. (This progress hasn't halted either, and now we have Mac OS X Lion 10.7, which supports icons up to 1,024 pixels in size!) What's more, esoteric tools like ResEdit were no longer needed, as icons could be created in the graphic editors that I used every day, like Illustrator and Photoshop.

The amount of detail possible also meant the process had become more time-consuming, creating multiple resolutions of the same image for different contexts such as file views and the Dock. It was no less enjoyable for that, though. As I had originally trained in illustration, but had so far followed a graphic design career path, icon design was a welcome return to my earlier skills. I started by creating replacements for the Camino browser's UI in 2003 and, in particular, its application icon, which I based on the famous Japanese painting *The Great Wave* by Hokusai.

Looking back now, those early icons were fairly low quality, but I was hooked and all I wanted to do was stop all these print and web design projects and instead draw icons all day.

It was the Great Wave icon for Camino that got the attention of Steven Garrity, who was charged with finding volunteers for a new Mozilla visual identity team to create a new identity for their new browser. Originally called Phoenix and then Firebird, it was eventually given the permanent name of Firefox for its first public release in 2004. We all came up with various ideas, but the fox with a fiery tail we decided on came from Daniel Burka, which was then sketched by Stephen Desroches, before I took it on and rendered it.

Strictly speaking, a firefox is a red panda (without doubt a very cute animal), but the European fox looked bolder and more iconic. The new icon was launched in early 2004, and since then Firefox has become a global brand and the icon has been updated further by the Iconfactory. It was a big leap in profile for me, and has allowed me to follow icon design projects ever since, for clients such as Skype, Opera and Linotype.

Icons as child's play

When our local primary school decided to run a creative arts month in 2007, parents whose profession was in the arts were invited to come in and run a workshop, demonstrating their skill and giving the children a chance to have a go. I decided that I could do one for icon design, although I would have to explain what icons were and why we need them. The children were fascinated to come to terms with the fact that icons are such an integral part of all their lives, even though they didn't realise it or know what they were called beforehand.

I started by handing out sheets with a 16×16 grid and asked them to plan what they would do for their first icon. While they could design anything they liked, most followed the suggestion of trying to sum themselves up in a icon, by showing their interests, for instance. We then used a free, open source application called LiquidIcon to create a simple .ico using the basic Windows colour palette. It was an ideal application to use, with a very simple grid interface that echoed the handout sheets they'd been working on.

The results were interesting. Most weren't interested at the start but, once they got going, everyone was engaged. The thing I noticed most was that there was a significant portion who understood how small the final icon would be, and how simple it needed to be.

The principles we'll explore in this book are the same — keep icons simple, clean and recognisable.

Further reading

Origin of the modern use of 'icon'

http://www.guidebookgallery.org/articles/ofmiceandmenus

A brief history of computer icons

http://psd.tutsplus.com/articles/theory/know-your-icons-part-1-a-brief-history-of-computer-icons/

A history of Windows Icons

http://www.windows-icons.com/history.htm

Gerd Arntz - the creative lead of the Isotype team

http://www.gerdarntz.org/isotype

Isotype Revisited

http://www.isotyperevisited.org/

Isotype Revisited is a three and a half year research project (2007—11) based in the *Department of Typography and Graphic Communication* at the *University of Reading*.

Designing the Xerox Star Workstation

http://www.guidebookgallery.org/articles/humanfactorstestinginthedesignofxeroxs8010starofficeworkstation

Why the push for the desktop metaphor?

http://www.guidebookgallery.org/articles/thedesktopenvironment

(Reprinted from Personal Computing, issue 8/1984, pp. 64-75.)

Symbol Sourcebook: An Authoritative Guide to International Graphic Symbols

Henry Dreyfuss

From Hieroglyphics to Isotype: A Visual Autobiography

Otto Neurath

Chapter 2

How we use icons

Icons are more than just decoration or pretty pictures. They serve a wide range of purposes, from overcoming language barriers and describing functions, to conveying mood and emotion. This chapter looks at the various uses of icons, but also covers an equally important aspect — when not to use them.

Now that we understand how modern icons came to be by looking at their origins and history, and how designers tend to get involved in icon creation, let's start to think in more detail about what purpose icons play in design. Even though the focus of this book is on icons for websites, and desktop and mobile applications, it is useful to consider the wider context: books, road signs, airports and railway stations, and anywhere else you see icons. In many cases, you've probably not consciously thought about the icons that influence you every day of your life, and the power they can have when used effectively.

Imagine software, like a graphics editor or media player, without any icons. Instead of play and pause buttons, or a tool palette, what if they just had text labels or a list of names like Airbrush, Pencil, Blur Tool…? They would still be usable, but our brains would have to process a lot more information, and the interface would have to be much larger to accommodate the text. This becomes crucial on mobile devices, which have much more restricted space to convey functions. Icons often support text labels in software, but they're just as often used on their own.

While icons are used for a wide range of tasks in software and the wider world, on the web they're often seen primarily as a means of decoration, a way of adding some visual interest to text. There's no harm in this, of course, and they can certainly serve that purpose well. Lists of features can be broken up and made more appealing by a representative icon, and this is very popular on sites for software in particular:

Icons are capable of so much more, though. When used thoughtfully, they can aid navigation, highlight important areas and provide feedback or instruction. Here are some examples.

User workflow

Let's first consider some different ways in which icons can be used to make our websites and applications more meaningful and easier to use for our users.

Functionality and navigation

As well as the obvious usage, that is, representing functions in toolbars and video player controls, icons can provide support for navigation.

At a glance, navigation text isn't easy to scan, especially if the text is all uppercase: there is too little visual difference to each label to make the desired section stand out. If you squint slightly, you can see this effect. Adding icons (or perhaps just one icon to highlight an important section such as a shopping basket) draws the user's attention, breaks up the outline and adds uniqueness that makes wayfinding faster. The big, bold icons used by the Mission Bicycle Company are my favourite examples of this:

Compare the top version with that on the bottom, where only text is used in the navigation — which one draws you in more and feels easier to navigate?

The Narhwal Company, which makes wallets and other products from recycled ties, use icons to great effect in their product categories rather than site sections:

Using icons in the first place can often be effective; size and clarity, however, are key to icons' usefulness in navigation. In the following example (with names changed to protect the innocent), the icons are the same height as the text's x-height, equally spaced between the labels (rather than closer to their corresponding label) and indistinct in themselves. It's hard to tell at a glance which icon belongs to which navigation label, or even what they are:

If it wasn't possible to use larger icons in the design, the navigation would have worked better without any icons at all.

The various sections of a site aren't necessarily what you will need to draw attention to though — it could be one particular section or function of the site. If it's an online shop, where are the shopping basket and the search field? If the site is for software, where is the download link or support section? We instinctively look for appropriate clues, and a well chosen icon (cart or basket, magnifying glass, downwards arrow, lifebelt or question mark) is quick to process.

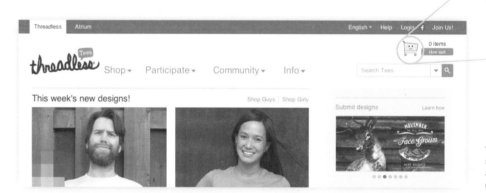

Threadless displays both search and shopping cart prominently, with the added personality of a cart that's sad until you put something in it

Vimeo is a great example of icon use on the web. The icons are not only clear and concise with a very consistent style, they're not overused (a problem we'll cover more later).

On Vimeo, the video sharing site, the homepage's key function is obvious — upload a video!

A video page in Vimeo shows other functions. Aside from the obvious video controls of play, pause and full screen, the ability to like, share or watch later is kept clearly within the context of the video:

National flags, in the form of icons, are often used as a way of navigating region-specific subsites or allowing the user to select their language. While this works well for the former, it doesn't work so well for the latter, since one flag might represent a multilingual country such as China or Belgium, or a language spoken in several different countries, like Spanish or French.

Managing expectations

Icons can also let the user know if something is going to happen when an item is selected. If we see a downwards arrow in navigation (also called a 'disclosure triangle' — perhaps the simplest icon of all), we expect a dropdown menu with more options to appear, rather than being taken somewhere else. Twitter uses this in several places:

On Twitter, the dropdown arrow is used in three different locations

The following example from the getflow.com website uses two different icons to let the user know what to expect when selecting the thumbnails. The first symbol, a magnifying glass, means you can expect to see a zoomed version of the image, whereas the play symbol indicates that a video will be shown instead:

 **Take a Tour**
See what makes Flow so great.

 **Flow for iPhone**
Available on the App Store.

 **Watch the Video**
See Flow in action.

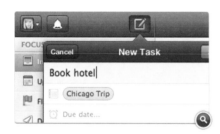

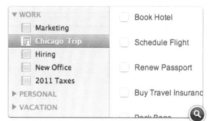

In the same way, icons can be used to show that a link will actually download a file, such as a PDF document or an .ics calendar feed (accompanied by its size if it's a large download so that the user can judge whether their connection can handle it).

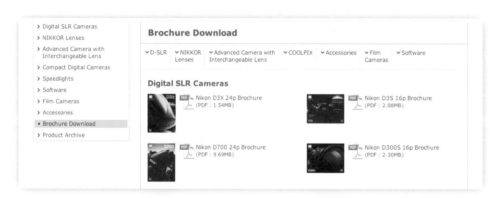

Comparisons

As well as making what could have been a boring chart look appealing, the use of feature icons on Jepco Mini Storage makes it easy to compare storage types at a glance, quicker than text alone:

In addition, the designer has taken the time to write `alt` text for each item. This ensures that, if for whatever reason the images aren't visible (images turned off, low bandwidth or a visually impaired screen reader user for example), the chart still makes sense:

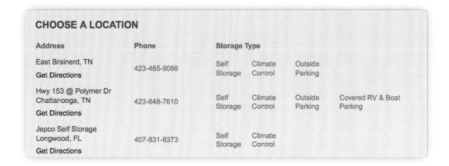

It's an easy thing to add, and should be a standard practice, but it's all too often overlooked.

Status and notifications

Chat applications embody the quintessential use of status icons, enabling us to see others' availability at a glance:

Status icons are useful in other contexts too. When updating files in Coda, there are five states associated with them:

1. Unsaved: The filename in the sidebar gets a simple circle to indicate there have been changes that haven't been saved yet.

2. Publish: Once the file is saved, it changes to a publish icon giving you a one-click means of uploading it.

3. Pending: Coda is connecting to the server (usually very brief).

4. Uploading: An animated clock icon shows the progress of the file upload, and the application icon in the Mac OS X dock adds a blue upload badge.

5. Finished: Once upload is complete, the dock icon gains a green tick mark badge.

css
- basic.css
- hicksmade.css
- ie7.css
- ie8.css
- layout.css ○ —————— Unsaved
- mediaqueries.css

- ie8.css
- layout.css ⬆ —————— Publish
- mediaqueries.css

- ie8.css
- layout.css ••• —————— Pending
- mediaqueries.css

- ie8.css
- layout.css ◕ —————— Uploading
- mediaqueries.css
- print.css
- typography.css

Dock Complete

- dev
- domains
- download
- favicon.ico
- feeds

Providing feedback

Another great use of icons is to provide feedback in response to user actions such as validating forms. It's best practice not to rely on colour alone to convey important information for two reasons:

- To avoid misunderstanding for people with colour-blindness. Even without colour-blindness, everyone sees colour slightly differently, so there's room for misinterpretation.

- Different cultures attribute different meanings to colours. While red conveys good luck (a positive interpretation) in China, it represents danger or warning (a negative interpretation) in the West. Icons can help reinforce the meaning.

We'll cover colour meanings in more depth in Chapter 4 when we look closely at the metaphors behind icons.

Often the default way to warn users of problems with a form they've filled in is simply to add error text in red or a red border around the relevant field. If colour alone isn't enough to convey the meaning, how can we improve that? In this signup form from grooveshark.com, you are given the option of creating a custom URL for your profile. If I enter a name that has already been taken, I'm immediately informed with a clear icon of a cross on a red circle:

The red suggests an error to those that can see it, but the icon makes it clear. Going one step further, you can give positive feedback too. Once I'd entered a name that wasn't previously taken, the icon changed to an affirming tick:

To make provision for these in your form design, it's best to position them on the same line as the relevant field to avoid ambiguity. Grooveshark's solution of placing them inside the field works because they've allowed plenty of padding in the text field.

Overcoming language barriers

Rather than having to provide multiple translations of the content, icons can summarise this information in a way that doesn't depend on language, which is particularly useful for wayfinding and signage.

In 1974, the United States Department of Transportation commissioned the American Institute of Graphic Arts (AIGA) to fix the confusing variety of symbols used in transportation hubs like airports and railway stations. As well as different metaphors, there were issues of age, culture and legibility to consider.

The team of AIGA designers led by Roger Cook and Don Shanosky undertook an exhaustive survey of pictograms already in use around the world, which drew from sources as diverse as Tokyo International Airport and the 1972 Olympic Games in Munich. By 1979, a total of fifty icons were devised.

These symbols are an International Standard (ISO 7001) and as such are widely used today; they can be downloaded as vector EPS artwork from the AIGA site. Finding internationally recognised symbols or objects isn't straightforward, however:

> *"Sun Microsystems learned their email package for an old product called SunView used an icon that confused people outside the United States. The icon was a US-style mailbox with a red flag that was raised and lowered to indicate the presence of new messages. Most people in other cultures had never seen a mailbox with a red flag and thus had no idea what it was supposed to mean. Never mind that the red flag metaphor was incorrectly applied even for a US audience. Since that time, most software and email providers have found opened and closed envelope icons to be more universally understood across cultures."*
>
> **'International symbol, icon blunders can be avoided', by Adam Wooten**

Wooten goes on to point out problems with other metaphors such as an owl, widely considered in the West to represent wisdom, but which actually means stupidity in parts of Asia.

McDonald's nutrition icons

An enormous challenge in cross-cultural communication was taken on by McDonald's when it redesigned its food packaging in 2007 as part of a 'Nutrition Information Initiative'. The aim was to make its nutrition information more understandable, but providing translations for each of the five categories (calories, protein, fat, carbs and salt) in all of its territories would have been out of the question, particularly when some of the 109 target countries encompass as many as ten languages each. There was also no existing iconography in this area, so a new cross-cultural visual language had to be developed from scratch.

Working with ENLASO, a company specialising in translation and localisation, and Boxer Design Consultants in the UK, a series of icon concepts was developed and iterated upon. Maxwell Hoffman from ENLASO outlined the four main challenges as:

25%		495kcal
36%		27g
37%		25g
15%		40g
46%		2.3g

- What visuals can communicate the desired nutrients?
- Does the visual work in 109 countries without evoking negative or socially and politically inappropriate connotations?
- Will the visuals print or display well in all media, including packaging, from paper to polystyrene?
- Does anyone else already own rights to the image that might prevent it from being used in this context?

During tests, the visuals were judged in each country on criteria such as: the possibility of negative connotations; possible legal issues; assessment of risk in misinterpretation; as well as whether they were simply recognisable. Just as the AIGA discovered with the Department of Transport icons, the metaphors used in icons can be too open to interpretation.

"Feedback was often surprising and sometimes even amusing. An image of a bone to represent calcium was rejected due to its regional association with dogs, while a simple abstract image of a four-leaved plant, symbolizing fibre, was interpreted as everything from a Christmas tree to marijuana!"
Maxwell Hoffmann, ENLASO

When gathering feedback on the iterations, one area of common ground that was discovered was the combination of yellow or orange and black being associated with traffic signs. This combination ended up being used for the fat icon.

While red did mean danger in the majority of the 109 countries, it was used for protein to be consistent with food pyramids, and so was a nutritional standard. As the icons are never meant to be used individually, the consensus was that the negative connotation of the colour was reduced when in the company of other icons.

The final challenge facing the design team was the medium the visuals would be used in. In some instances they would be printed small, in a single colour and on to styrofoam. This meant that the style had to be bolder and simpler than the earlier iterations. No fine detail could be used, as this would be lost as the ink bled:

An incredible amount of work has gone into developing these icons, so as well as being used in their packaging, McDonald's has made the results freely available to other food and restaurant industries worldwide to help them become a recognised standard. It takes a large company (like McDonald's) to really ensure symbols are widely propagated. The wider their reach, the more effective they will become.

Expressing emotion

As well as substituting written language, we also use icons as a shorthand to convey emotion and tone of voice in media where messages are necessarily short and hastily written, such as text chat or forums. These emoticons started life as combinations of letters to form sideways representations of facial expressions — such as ;-p — but now many applications will replace these with the corresponding emoticon. As well as conveying mood, they can also communicate tone. The tone of many a potentially insulting paragraph is changed with a wink at the end.

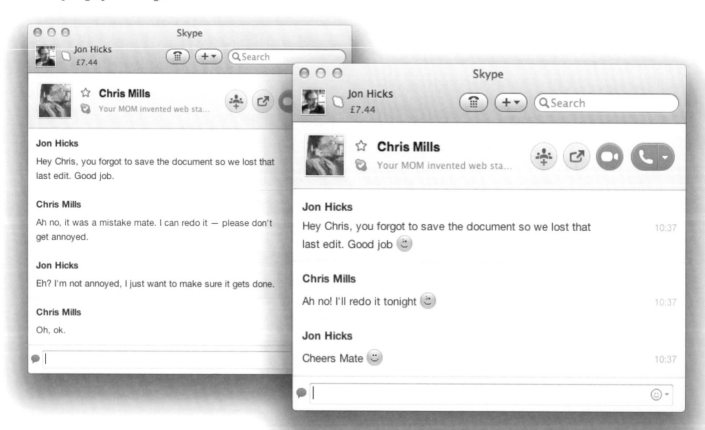

Nowhere are emoticons more used than in Japan. They call them emoji (絵文字), a combination of e (絵) 'picture' + moji (文字) 'letter'. They go beyond facial expressions to include objects such as food and hand gestures. It even has a standardised Unicode set of 722 characters.

New Skype emoticons

With millions of users worldwide, Skype Chat's emoticons are very widely recognised. Originally designed by Priidu Zilmer when he joined the Skype visual design team in 2004, Hicksdesign and animator Julian Frost were commissioned to update the emoticon set in 2011, and create multiple sizes.

The original emoticons only existed as 19×19px and, while they had transparent backgrounds, the edges were aliased. An odd-numbered grid can allow you to centre elements better (see chapter 5), but the decision was taken to start at 20px to allow more straightforward scaling to 30, 40, 60 and 80px sizes, as well as design some new (hidden) icons. This meant some of the basic proportions of the eyes to head had to be changed.

Original 19px Smiley   **Updated 20px Smiley**

As the current emoticon set was widely recognised, the updated icons couldn't stray too far from the originals.

The core of the Skype emoticons are based on the familiar text emoticons, but some required more study of facial expressions. This was where the cameras built in to modern computers came in useful, providing a quick source of reference.

As part of the redesign, Zilmer's hidden icon was updated too

Like emoji, the Skype emoticons also contain some more unusual representations. The bow emoticon is particularly important for the Japanese audience and, in order to express the correct emotion, the hands needed to be folded in front of the figure. In the West, we might expect the hands to be by the sides, but in Japan this conveys disappointment, tiredness and even 'want to die (hanging)'. Hands folded in front is warm and sincere.

While having the hands at the sides looks more correct to those in the West, the hands folded in front conveys warmth and sincerity

I talked to Mark McLaughlin, the design lead for mobile at Skype, about their side of the process...

How many Skype users are there worldwide?

" Skype had 170 million average monthly connected users for the three months ending 30 June 2011. This excludes users connected via our joint venture partners.

How long has Skype had its current emoticons, and what was the reason for the change?

" Emoticons have been in Skype since the earliest versions of our Windows application, the first appearance of which was an internal build from way back in May 2004. Back then we had just ten in total:

The 19-pixel versions had been working out great for years on our desktop applications, but when it came to mobile phones and tablets with touch interfaces and ever increasing screen pixel densities, it was clear that temporary fixes like pixel-doubling them wasn't going to be sustainable — even more so with the introduction of the iPhone 4's Retina display.

The bow icon from the smallest (20px) to the largest (80px) notice how details like the hands become just straight rectangles on the smallest version

Do you see variation in how different cultures perceive and use emoticons?

> *The great thing about them is that they transcend language — they're essentially universal. The most common difference in usage of one of our emoticons seems to be bow, which is a genuinely essential part of etiquette and communication when working with our Japanese employees and partners.*

What is the story behind the hidden emoticons in Skype?

> *A few like toivo are tributes to former staff who've made a significant contribution during their time at Skype; others like poolparty are references to amusing incidents at Skype events (you had to be there, I'm told); most of the others are ones we wanted to keep in because they're fun, but were probably a little inappropriate to expose in the main emoticon picker.*

Do you have a personal favourite?

> *I rarely have a need to use it, but the emo with his fringe always gives me a giggle.*

Icons as souvenirs

In gaming, the concept of collecting trophies and achievement icons has been around for a while, but it's a fairly recent development on the web. Users of location-based social networks like Foursquare and Gowalla gain stamps and pins as part of sharing their location and the story of what they're doing there. The original version of Gowalla went further with the concept of items, icons of objects like books and food that could be collected or dropped at locations. Icons had become rewards, but the focus has changed to being a social guide.

It may not be everyone's idea of fun, but I personally get a real thrill from well-illustrated stamps like the famous Beatles album cover location at Abbey Road. As well as becoming souvenirs of the places I have visited, they give me a flavour of the places I haven't (yet).

Gowalla

The Gowalla team had previously been known for the Facebook game Pack Rat, and Firewheel Design, a studio specialising in icon design. I talked to Gowalla's founder, Josh Williams, about how they use icons and the process of creating them.

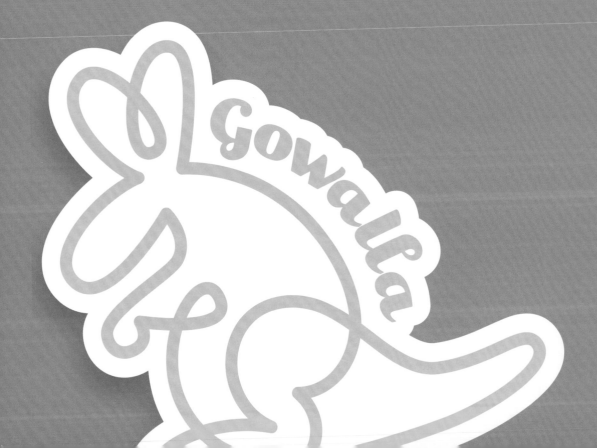

Where did the idea of Gowalla come from and, in particular, the use of icons?

Gowalla came from a love of travel and a desire to share amazing moments with people close to you. Capturing those places with beautiful icons, similar to passport stamps, was an obvious choice, especially with our team's background in iconography.

How many artists are involved?

We have three in-house illustrators, Brian Brasher (@etherbrian), Akab Defibaugh (@AlanDefibaugh) and John Marstall (@iconmaster) who have created over 1,000 icons representing the world's most interesting places, from Wrigley Field to Stonehenge to the Grand Palace in Bangkok.

Do you think the common human compulsion to collect is a driving force with Gowalla users or is it more to share your current location for social reasons?

Everyone experiences Gowalla in a unique way but, for most, it's the social travel guide aspect that makes it unique. The stamps are lovely mementos as well as a way for us to highlight extraordinary places.

What was the process behind the distinctive Gowalla icon style, and how do you maintain it across a team of artists?

The thick borders and bold colors of the Gowalla stamp style have been part of our style since our days as a small design studio. Graphics full of RGB goodness is where we came from, so we wanted places in Gowalla to provide a rich visual reward. Even the generic stamps (those not created specifically for a certain building or landmark or natural wonder) are generic in name only.

Maintaining the Gowalla aesthetic has been fairly simple. Each of the artists is very talented and works well within the boundaries of our simple style guide. Everyone sees the finished product before it goes live, which makes it easy to catch anything out of the ordinary, as well as open the door to conversations about technique.

How long do the icons take to produce, and what do you use to create them?

" As you would imagine, the time involved varies widely. Passport stamps include everything from logos to intricate renderings of the world's finest buildings. The average time is about two hours for each icon.

Our artists primarily use Illustrator.

Do you have a favourite stamp or pin?

" It was insanely difficult to choose, so here are fifteen favourites:

Everything in moderation

While icons have a wide range of uses, it's not always the right solution to use them, and it's easy to go overboard and use them to draw attention to every little detail. At least, I find it very easy to do so!

When trying to decide whether an icon is necessary, the first step is always to remove it and see if it works well enough without it. If it does enhance the content or interface in one of the ways covered in this chapter, then it's earning its keep.

I also consider the following points:

- Is it merely being used for decoration, to break up the text and make the design more appealing? Or does it serve a purpose beyond that?

- Is the icon repeated so many times that it has lost its meaning or purpose?

- Are there too many in a small space? A classic example of icon overuse is the ubiquitous list of options for 'Share this!'.

Bookmark and Share
 More »

Fortunately, this is a trend on the decline.

- Does the icon need supporting text to make it understandable? Is it possible that the concept being communicated is just too abstract or unfamiliar to work as an icon? In Chapter 4 we'll look at the process of choosing the metaphor.

- Is the overwhelming feeling of the page or interface like a Christmas tree? If so, try monochrome icons. Do the icons still convey the same meaning? Or, if every navigation element has its own icon, try it with just the most important one, such as the shop or shopping basket, or perhaps the contact details or where to find us information.

The design of 37 Signals' Basecamp web application has been much copied, but one of the elements that its derivatives miss is its restraint with icons. The interface is not littered with icons — just key functions like delete, print and add.

Summary

Now that we've looked at all the ways in which icons can be used beyond simple adornment, we can move on to actually creating them...

Chapter references

International symbol, icon blunders can be avoided
http://www.deseretnews.com/article/705370663/International-symbol-icon-blunders-can-be-avoided.html

AIGA icons for the Department of Transport
http://www.aiga.org/symbol-signs/

McDonald's Nutrition Icons:
http://www.translationdirectory.com/articles/article1387.php
http://www.boxercreative.co.uk/our_work/mcdonalds_nutrition.html

Skype
http://www.telecompaper.com/news/skype-grows-fy-revenues-20-reaches-663-mln-users
http://hicksdesign.co.uk/journal/new-skype-emoticons
http://julianfrost.co.nz/things/skype-emoticons/

Chapter 3

Favicons

Now we'll start building up our icon skills, beginning with favicons. Even if you've never created any other types of icons before, I'm willing to bet that everyone reading this has at some point made a favicon. For the majority of you, it's probably a regular task. They're an ideal place to start, as we can look at ways of achieving pixel-crisp artwork and clarity at small sizes — skills that we'll build on in later chapters.

"A logo is a flag, a signature, an escutcheon, a street sign. A logo does not sell (directly), it identifies."

Paul Rand

Favicons (also called shortcut icons) first appeared in Internet Explorer 5, where placing a favicon.ico icon in the root of a website would cause a 16px square image to appear next to the URL in the address bar and in bookmark lists, without requiring any HTML. Initially this had the added benefit of estimating how many times our sites were bookmarked by counting requests for the favicon, but this is no longer reliable since browsers started supporting the favicon for more than just bookmarks.

The difference between favicons and the kind of icons we'll tackle in the application icons chapter, is that there's no deliberation over the correct metaphor here. Their purpose isn't to summarise an action or overcome language barriers, but to represent the site as a signpost and extend its branding into the browser. As such, it will almost always be a smaller version of the site's logo. Fortunately, it is generally simpler to re-create a logo in sixteen pixels than an application icon.

While much larger sizes can also be used these days, a 16px version is essential and an ideal place to start if you're new to designing icons. The skills you pick up from creating them will serve as the basis for the other types we'll be looking at later. If you can achieve clarity at this size, the rest will fall into place.

Even if you've never created any of the other types of icons discussed in this book, I'm willing to bet that everyone reading this has at some point made a favicon and, for the majority of you, that it's a regular task.

Before you start

Before we start creating any icon, we need to know how and where it will be used, as that will affect how we create and deploy it. The subsections below will cover the different considerations:

- What is the context?
- What sizes are needed?
- Which formats are needed?

What is the context?

A favicon could appear on a variety of backgrounds, so we will need to use transparency to get the best option to fit all. It won't always be displayed on a white address bar background — it may appear on Windows Aero glass, a grey Mac OS X UI, or a dark browser theme. Firefox 4 also adds a grey button background to favicons in its address bar; it is set slightly larger so it will always border the favicon.

What sizes are needed?

If you were to create a favicon for every possible use, the sizes you would need to create are:

- 16px: For general use in all browsers, could be displayed in the address bar, tabs or bookmarks views
- 24px: Toolbar favicon in Internet Explorer 9
- 32px: New tab page in Internet Explorer, Pinned Site in Windows 7+ and Safari's 'Read Later' sidebar
- 57px: Standard iOS home screen (iPod Touch, iPhone first generation to 3G)
- 72px: iPad home screen icon
- 96px: Favicon used by the GoogleTV platform
- 114px: iPhone 4+ home screen icon (twice the standard size for the retina display)
- 128px: Chrome Web Store
- 256x160px: Opera Speed Dial

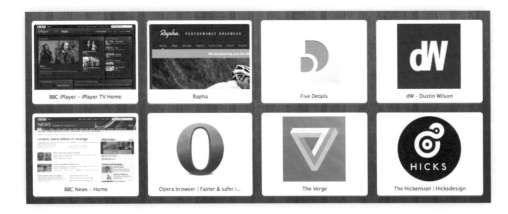

Opera Speed Dial

Chrome Web Store

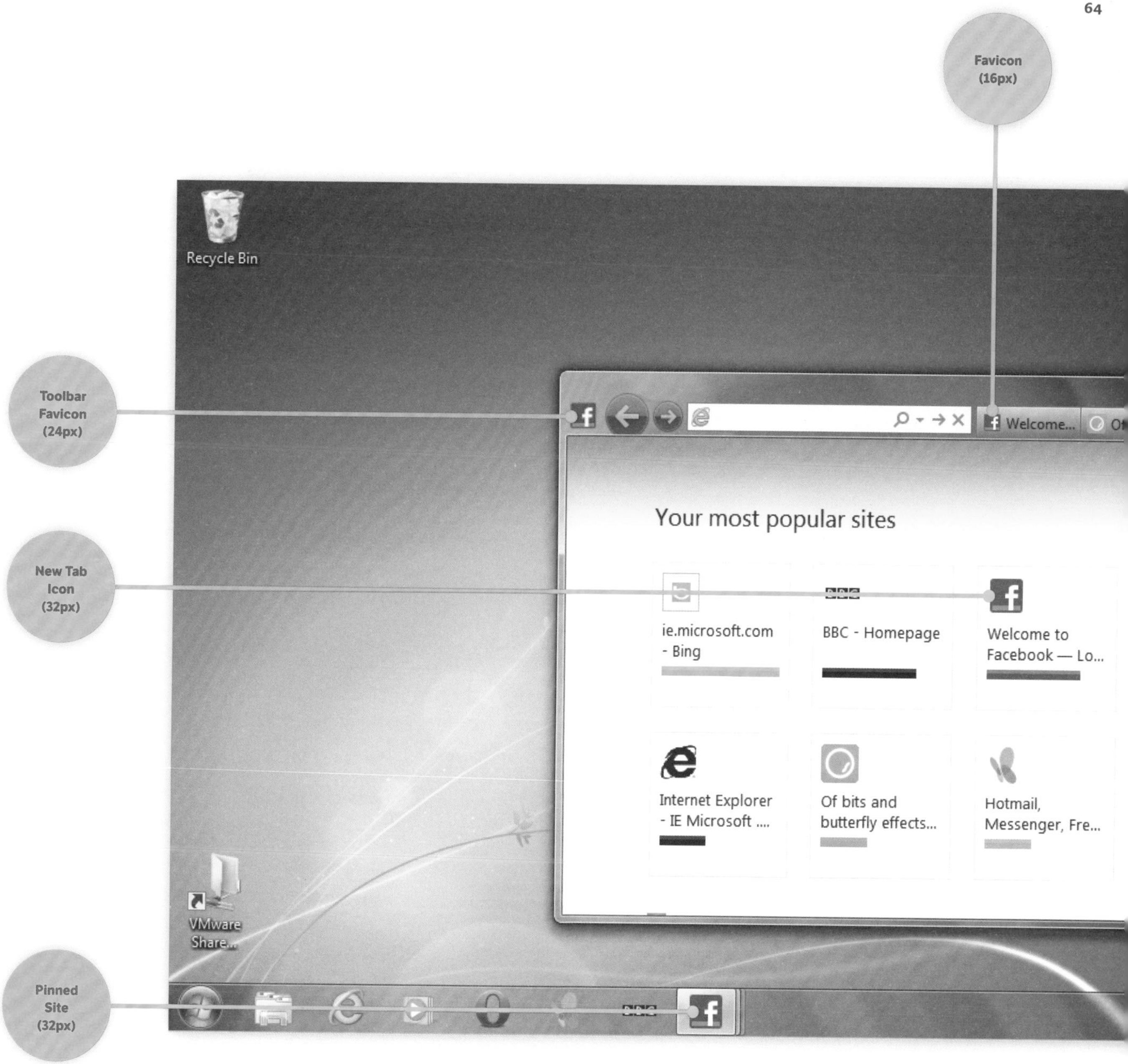

Favicon
(16px)

Toolbar
Favicon
(24px)

New Tab
Icon
(32px)

Pinned
Site
(32px)

Recycle Bin

VMware
Share...

Welcome...   O Of

Your most popular sites

ie.microsoft.com
- Bing

BBC - Homepage

Welcome to
Facebook — Lo...

Internet Explorer
- IE Microsoft ....

Of bits and
butterfly effects...

Hotmail,
Messenger, Fre...

57px and 114px favicons in iOS   **96px favicon in Google TV**

Do we really need to supply all of these? As always, it depends on context. A site for a Mac and iOS software company would benefit from the various iPad and iPhone specific icons, whereas an intranet site that will only be displayed in Internet Explorer would be better off with a multi-resolution ICO file. A web app, designed to be viewed on mobile and desktop would benefit from spending the time creating all of these sizes.

While it is possible to use a 32px icon that can be reduced by 50% to 16px (for example, by using 2px strokes that will reduce neatly to 1px), this relies on the browser to scale it, and it may crop it instead. It'll also result in a larger file, and we want to keep the favicon files as small as possible.

However, a really good compromise is to supply a 16px icon and one large size icon, such as 128px, that would be ideal for large uses such as the Chrome Web Store and Opera's Speed Dial. While a 128px image resized to 57px won't look as good as a bespoke, optimised 57px image (as it doesn't reduce evenly — 44.5%), it may be satisfactory for your needs. In fact, this is exactly what Apple does: it only supplies one more icon other than the favicon, an apple-touch-icon.png icon sized at 129px. What's good enough for Apple...

Whatever you decide to do, at the very minimum a 16px icon is essential to avoid the browser default icon. Safari displays an attractive blue globe, but most will simply show a blank document icon.

If you don't include a basic 16px favicon, it's a lost opportunity to extend the brand of the site beyond the page itself. A missing favicon.ico file also causes problems on high traffic sites, as the server will generate a 404 error for every first request. Firefox remembers sites that are missing a favicon and doesn't re-request them, but it's the only browser that does this.

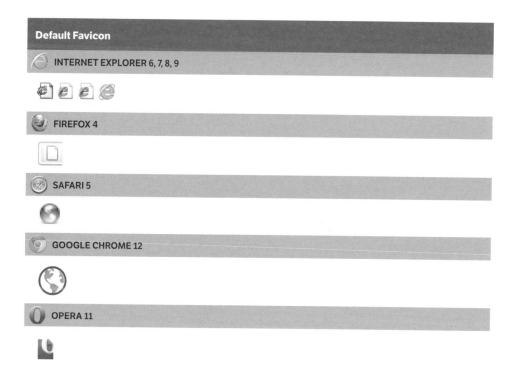

Which formats are needed?

In the early days, when a Windows ICO format was the only file type supported, there was a little timesaving trick we could rely on — save a favicon as a 16×16 GIF and simply rename it, giving it a .ico file extension. It was a hack, but it worked! Nowadays, we don't need to and shouldn't use this method as tools for creating an ICO file are more readily and freely available online. In addition, other formats are now supported for favicon usage, although there are essentially only two formats worth considering:

- The ICO file is still the most widely supported. Unlike PNG it can contain multiple resolutions and bit-depths, which is very useful on Windows. Internet Explorer uses favicons in a variety of sizes, such as the 32-pixel icon for the Windows 7 taskbar, and an ICO is the only way to offer these. It's also the only format that is detected without using a `<link>` element.

- PNG can be more convenient, however, as it doesn't require any special tools to create, it supports alpha transparency and gives us the smallest possible file size. Its only drawback is that Internet Explorer doesn't support it (it only accepts ICO).

As for the other options:

- GIF and animated GIF offer no advantages other than support for very old browsers.
- JPG is an unlikely choice, even if the image is a photo. It lacks the crispness of PNG, and you won't see any benefit from its better blends at such a small size.
- SVG would be excellent if more browsers supported it for favicon use, but only Opera does currently.
- There is also a cheeky little subformat of PNG — APNG (animated PNG) — supported by Firefox and Opera, but its usefulness is questionable. An animated favicon just looks irritating and needy.

Drawing at 16 pixels

Now we've looked at the background information and preparation for creating favicons, let's get our hands dirty and start drawing some icons.

Tools

This handbook doesn't presume to know what graphics editor you prefer to use, as tools are very much a personal choice. What works for me won't necessarily work for you! Whatever app you use, though, it must allow you to create vector artwork with a pixel preview, rather than just smooth high resolution. It's also helpful if it lets you see a pixel grid, making it easier to draw and plan the icon. With 16px icons in particular, you'll want to make sure that straight edges are kept within the grid, as anything halfway will make the icon appear blurred:

As you can see, this is particularly noticeable on shapes with straight edges, and can make the artwork less recognisable.

My personal preference is Adobe Illustrator CS5, so this is what you will see in the examples. It won't refer to any Illustrator-specific features, however. The appendix lists the most common applications that you might use, from the expensive to the free and open source.

Getting busy with the drawing

All being well, before we start we'll be provided with a vector file of the logo (.ai or, more commonly, .eps) that we want to 'favicon-ise'. I say 'all being well' as I've lost count of the number of corporations that drag a logo.gif file off their site and tell the designer, "There's the logo file you need…"!

No matter how complex the logo is, we don't want to replicate too many details in the favicon. Simple is best. For example, AT&T's logo has complex transparency effects, but for the 16px favicon, this is reduced to simple lines.

Case study

Five Details favicons

Five Details designs and develops software for Mac, iPhone and iPad. For this company with more than 100,000 users of its Flow and Seamless apps, and an Apple Design Award under its belt, Hicksdesign created the Five Details logo, branding and website.

○ ○ ○   Five Details

◄ ► + http://fivedetails.com/| ⟳ Q▾ Google

seamless
your music, to go.

With one tap, Seamless fades your
music, podcast, or audiobook out on
your Mac, and in on your iPhone (or
vice-versa)

For our example workflow, we'll be taking our original vector file and creating a 16px favicon from it, as well as the other sizes for the website. As Five Details focuses on Mac software, the context for this is going to mean a heavy emphasis on Mac desktop browsers and iOS mobile devices. It's worth spending time, therefore, making sure the full range of optimised Apple Touch icons are created as well: 57px for iPhone and iPod Touch, 72px for the iPad and 114px for the iPhone 4's Retina display.

In Illustrator, I've set up an artboard for each icon size. I prefer being able to see each size, side by side, rather than have an individual file for each. The artboards are named with their intended filename (such as 'favicon' or 'apple-touch-icon-114x114-precomposed') as this will be used when exporting with the script provided at *http://iconhandbook.co.uk/*

downloads/. We'll begin by resizing the artwork to 16px and seeing what we get. If the original happens to be a neat multiple of 16, then we'll be off to a good start, but it's more likely that it will need to be tweaked or redrawn from scratch, possibly even as pixel art (drawing each pixel individually) to ensure clarity. That isn't as daunting or time-consuming as it sounds, though!

If the image needs to include a background (as the Five Details icon does), then any padding that you need will reduce the size

Resizing even a simple logo to 16px shows that it needs further work to make it crisp

of the actual logo even further. While your icon doesn't require a background, it might help to control its contrast in a variety of environments. A simple grey favicon might look nice and subtle in a white address bar (bottom right), but when displayed on a grey tab in a Mac browser such as Firefox, it's easily lost (top right).

The two solutions to this are: to use transparent black (rather than grey) to allow it to darken proportionally in relation to it's background or add a coloured background to the favicon that will suit all circumstances. In this case, I felt it would have more strength on top of a light grey box background, with 3 pixels of padding on each side, which reduces the actual logo size to just 10px:

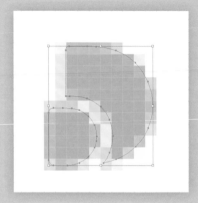

Unfortunately the edges don't fall neatly on to full pixels, and the gap between the two parts of the logo is almost closed up. In some cases we can tweak the anchor points of the path to make it sit on the pixel grid properly. If your chosen graphics editor supports pixel snapping (where it snaps the path you're editing to the pixel grid) then you'll find that you need to alternate this on and off for different tasks: for snapping straight edges it's very useful, but editing curves (such as the right side of the logo) is easier if it's off. Sometimes we'll want the path to sit halfway between pixels, not just for curves, but to deliberately create softer edges for elements such as shadows.

In this case, however, the simple shapes are easier to re-create in vectors from scratch. This at least gives the right proportions to help us re-create it. Placing the reduced artwork in separate layers and locking it allows us to use it as a guide, working on top of it.

It may be that we have to take some liberties with the logo proportions to get it to work, but 16px is very forgiving, and crisp artwork looks better than precision. If the shape still isn't working, we can try redrawing it in single pixels, either with bitmap tools like a pencil or preferably with vector rectangles, and then create our own anti-aliasing by changing the opacity of single pixels (in this case 1px square vector rectangles) where you want smooth edges:

Changing the opacity of single pixels

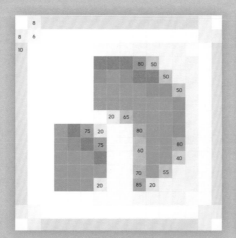
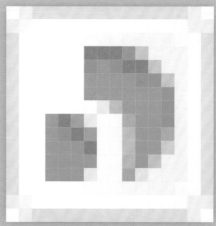

This gives us very fine control over the smoothness of curves, but is obviously rather fiddly. We'll have to zoom out often to see how the effect looks at actual size. Now we have the crisp silhouette, we can move on to adding other subtle elements such as inner shadow and white highlight at the bottom edges, all helping to visually sharpen the edges:

The border has been accentuated by adding an inner highlight — a 50% white stroke that is just enough to provide contrast, making the edge feel crisper. Some applications like Illustrator and Opacity allow you to add multiple strokes to the same vector object. For those that don't, you would need to make sure that you reduce the rounded corner radius to suit. For example, if the outside border had a radius of 4px, the inner highlight radius would need to be 3px to look correct.

Transparency is worth considering, as both ICO and PNG files support it. Assuming that this favicon will always be viewed on a white background would mean specifying a light grey border for our Five Details favicon:

The lightness of the border stops it being too distracting from the main element — the logo. However, we will not always view this on a white background, and when viewed on other backgrounds, the border jars badly:

An example dark background, IE9 with an Aero Glass nature theme

Instead of a 20% grey, using a black at 20% opacity would allow the border to blend in with the background and sit more comfortably:

Other favicon gotchas

Our favicon artwork is now finished, but there are other pitfalls to avoid.

It's best not to try to reproduce any perspective as this will reduce the icon's visual weight and require more anti-aliased pixels, making edges appear less crisp. Notice how the Reeder app website changes the isometric box logo to use a side-on perspective for the favicon. It's clear and still recognisable as the Reeder app.

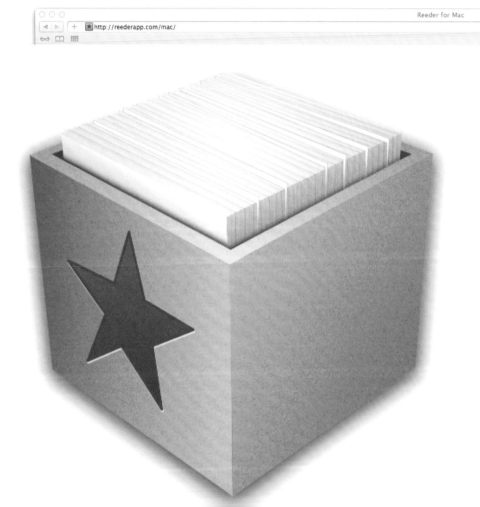

It might also be the case that the logo's proportions aren't square, and that it's too complex to reproduce in 16px. To get around this, select a strong element of the logo rather than attempting to show the whole thing. Mailchimp does this, focusing on Freddie the Chimp's head, rather than the whole chimp or logotype:

There are always exceptions, though, and despite your best efforts the logo and restrictive size is against you from the start. The BBC favicon is a good example of a logo that doesn't scale easily to a favicon, but also can't be reduced to a selected element without losing the brand. The white space top and bottom reduces its visual weight compared to other favicons, thereby diluting its importance.

However, this particular favicon highlights another potential issue with multiple ICO files. While the favicon.ico file contains both a 16px and 32px optimised icon, versions of Safari (before 5.1) display the 32px icon and reduce it to 16px, creating a unrecognisable mush:

Older versions of Safari (before 5.1) display the 32px icon at 16px

The correct size favicon shows in Firefox

The only way to avoid this is to add a 16px PNG favicon as well and add the `<link>` element to the HTML.

Exporting

If we're just making PNGs then this stage is straightforward, but creating the ICO requires a few more steps. There are many free online tools which will take a PNG and create an ICO for you (see appendix), or you can export it as one directly from Photoshop.

If you want to create an ICO with multiple resolutions, however, such as the 32px that Windows 7 uses for the taskbar, you will need more specialist software such as Iconbuilder, a plugin by the Iconfactory to be used in Photoshop or Fireworks. Iconbuilder comes with templates ready to place your artwork in, such as the Windows one here:

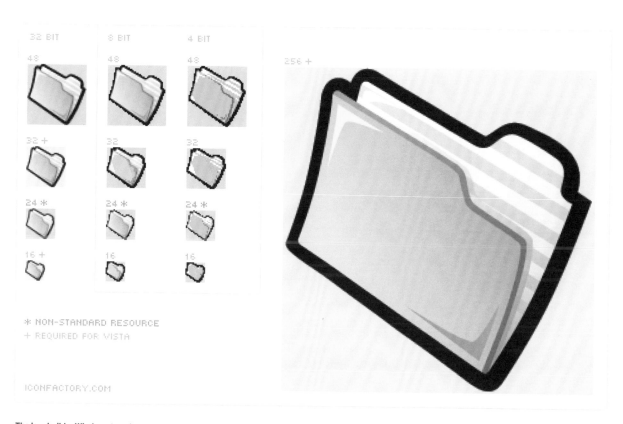

The Iconbuilder Windows template comes with all the sizes needed for application icons, but you can delete these, and just use the 16px and (optionally) 32px

With all the artwork in the correct box on the icon layer, we can then go to Iconbuilder (via Filters) and choose the Windows preset. Press Build and check each size looks correct in the preview window:

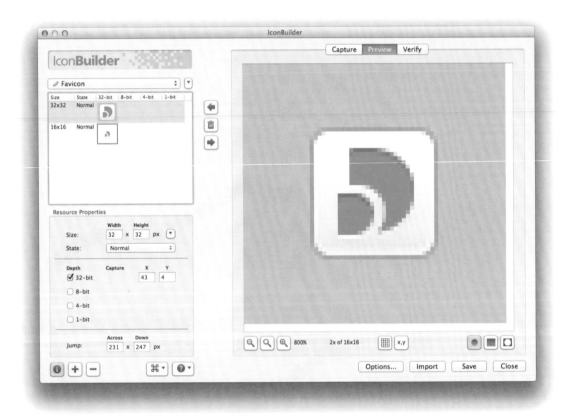

Any sizes or colour depths that aren't needed can be removed in the sidebar. If all looks good, we can then save as an ICO. Iconbuilder can also export in other formats at the same time, such as a set of PNGs for each resolution — very handy.

Implementation

For any format other than ICO, we need to point to it using the `<link>` element in the `<head>` of each page, with the appropriate `rel` and `type` attributes:

```
<link rel="icon" type="image/png" href="/pathto/favicon.png" />
```

This also allows us to change the favicon on sites we don't host, such as Tumblr or Blogger. Note that favicons don't need to be named favicon.ico or kept in the root of the site or application, but make sure you use the `<link>` element, otherwise the browser will be making multiple requests to try and find it.

Creating other types of favicon

As favicons tend to be left to the last minute, you may feel that there isn't time to create any of the larger sizes in the list. It's worth considering adding at least one more, though, as there is an increasing number of platforms that benefit from a larger favicon. In this section we'll discuss how to go beyond the 16px favicon, and complete the extended icon set for our Five Details example case study.

Apple Touch icons

Ever since the first iPhone, iOS (as the iPhone/iPod/iPad operating system is now known) has supported Apple Touch icons, a larger favicon that is used when a site is added to the home screen.

Apple Touch Icons, default (left) and precomposed (right) to prevent the gloss overlay

If we don't specify one for our site, iOS will just use a reduced screenshot of the page instead, which is hardly ever desirable.

Just like with favicon.ico files, we can add a file named apple-touch-icon.png to the root of our site, and iOS will discover it without needing a reference via a `<link>` element. We can also add an icon named apple-touch-icon-precomposed.png to the root; then iOS will use it without adding the gloss overlay, allowing more control.

iOS will also look for the appropriate size icon for the device first; Mobile Safari on iPad will look for icons named like so:

```
apple-touch-icon-72x72-precomposed.png
apple-touch-icon-72x72.png
```

We should supply these icons, if we have the time.

So we can specify the various size icons for different iOS devices without any extra HTML. Android OS (2.1+) doesn't support this, but it can make use of the precomposed Apple Touch icons if we point to them using `<link>` elements:

```
<link rel="apple-touch-icon-precomposed" href="apple-touch-icon-precomposed.png">
```

Android 2.2+ supports any Apple Touch icon, not just precomposed.

The value of the `rel` attribute here is proprietary to Apple, whereas everyone else uses just `icon`. In tandem with the `sizes` attribute, it also allows you to specify other sizes for iPad and the iPhone 4's Retina display:

```
<!-- For iPhone 4 Retina display: -->
<link rel="apple-touch-icon-precomposed" sizes="114x114" href="apple-touch-icon-114x114-precomposed.png">
<!-- For iPad: -->
<link rel="apple-touch-icon-precomposed" sizes="72x72" href="apple-touch-icon-72x72-precomposed.png">
```

Icons are listed largest first, so that iOS prior to version 4.2 (which doesn't support the `sizes` attribute) gets the correct icon. Other than Android, Apple Touch icons are also used by apps such as Reeder on the iPad.

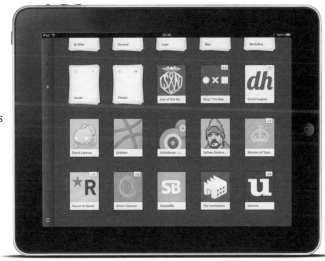

Opera Speed Dial

Another example of an app that supports the use of Apple Touch icons is the Opera browser's Speed Dial feature. Opera was the first browser to show thumbnails of the user's favourite websites when they open a new tab (nine by default, but you can change the settings to display more):

With version 11, this was extended further, allowing website owners the opportunity to specify any size icon between a minimum of 114×114px up to a maximum of 256×160px (making use of their landscape shape), using the `<link>` tag and filename:

```
<!-- Opera speed dial icon -->
<link rel="icon" type="image/png" href="195x195image.png">
```

Again, this can be more desirable than a thumbnail of the site and looks splendid. Finally, when testing, it's worth knowing that you can right-click a Speed Dial and choose Reload to make Opera get the latest version. It will always be shown with a white border and, depending on window size and number of Speed Dials, the icon itself won't always be displayed at full size.

Drawing the larger icons

Going back to our artboards in Illustrator and starting with the largest, we create the 114px icon. This will be seen at half the size on the iPhone 4's Retina display, which is twice the resolution of the original iPhone screen but has the same physical dimensions. So if we want a stroke to appear as 1px on screen, we'll need to draw it as 2px. However, 1px will still be visible, and we may prefer the lighter line weight in some contexts. Alternatively, if you're working in Photoshop, you can keep it at 1px and add a 50% inner glow of the stroke colour to achieve a compromise.

The only way to be sure is to test on the device. I can recommend the iOS app Review for testing this easily, but we can also test by increasing the canvas size of the image to 640×960px and importing to the iPhone via the built-in Photos app.

It's also worth bearing in mind that any transparent areas in the artwork will appear black (so custom iOS backgrounds will not show through). Don't include any rounded corners in your artwork, as these are added by iOS. However, it may be useful to know the radius of the corners and how they will affect it. Refer to the icon reference chart in the appendix for the various sizes, and the iOS icon template in the downloadable pack to preview your icon with rounded corners and gloss overlay.

This artwork can then be resized to 50% and used as the basis of the 57px artwork. If your calculations are correct, this shouldn't need any optimising, and should fall on the pixel grid exactly. Traditionally, icon sizes are neat doubles of each other: 16px → 32px (×2) → 64px (×2) and so on. This isn't the case with the iPad icon, at 72px. Again, take the largest size, and resize and optimise this, rather than vice versa, for the best results.

This part of the process is similar to that of creating application icons for various OSes, which is covered in more detail in Chapter 7.

Finally, to export each artboard as a PNG, use the script provided at *http://iconhandbook. co.uk/downloads/*. We now have four correctly named and sized PNG files in the root of our site.

Summary

At a bare minimum, we should always include a 16px favicon.ico file with our website, rather than leave it up to the browser to use its default icon. It not only looks good: it also strengthens our branding, and sticking with the ICO format ensures that Internet Explorer can make use of the icon.

Not including a 16px favicon means the browser default is associated with your site instead and it increases HTTP requests, a problem that is amplified on high-traffic sites.

While it may not be necessary to create all the icon sizes suggested in this chapter, it's definitely worth creating a large version favicon as well, such as 128px, which could then be resized to provide icons for different devices like the iPhone 4, as well as suiting uses such as the Chrome Web Store and Opera's Speed Dial.

Now that we've covered the basics with a 16px favicon, we can move on and create more interesting icons!

Chapter 4

The metaphor

The heart of an icon is the metaphor it uses, the functionality implied by the visual representation. This chapter starts as all projects do, with a client brief. We'll pick up this brief and run with it, working through the process of discovering if icon conventions already exist, and how to create them if they don't.

The metaphor

"When you're desperate for an idea — some icons, like the piece of paper, are no problem; but others defy the visual, like "undo". You look at things like hobo signs, like this: "Man with a gun lives here." Now, I can't say that anything in this book [Symbol Sourcebook (Dreyfuss)] is exactly transported into the Macintosh interface, but I think I got a lot of help from this, just thinking. This kind of symbol appeals to me because it had to be really simple, and clear to a group of people who were not going to be studying these for years in academia.[...] I still use it, and I'm grateful for it."

Susan Kare

Favicons are simply logos reduced to a small size and, as such, a very small part of the icon universe. With the exception of application icons (which we'll look at in the final chapter) the rest can be summarised as representations of either a tool, a function or a direction, depicted as either pictograms, ideograms or arbitrary symbols. These are the kind of icons you'll find on signage, navigation, and the interfaces of media players and applications. It's also the area where you might have bought a royalty-free icon set, and discovered that it doesn't contain everything you need.

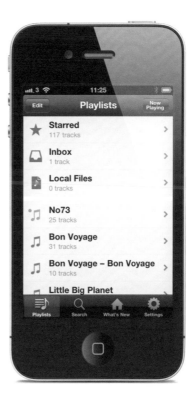

The Spotify app for iOS is a good example of icons used in navigation as well as media controls contexts

Before any drawing can take place, and whether you're starting from scratch or creating your own addition in the style of an existing set, the first stage of the process of creating icons is to consider the metaphor. How are you going to best represent that tool, function or direction?

The brief

The starting point of designing any icon is the brief — whether the request has come from the client, or you've decided yourself that it needs to be created. An icon brief is usually not much more than a laundry list of concepts, such as:

- Dashboard
- Print
- Compare
- Tasks
- Save

The concepts can vary from the self-explanatory to the undecipherable. In particular, I often find myself confronted with a large list of required icons for a website project, where every navigation item, menu, call-out box and feature description has been specified as needing an icon. As we've already seen in Chapter 2, this can be counter-productive to their effectiveness, distracting or even confusing for the user.

It's not the client's job to know exactly what they need to ask for, of course — it's your job to look at the context for each icon and advise them of the best approach and fit. Assessing each icon request needn't be a lengthy process, but there are a few questions I consider when evaluating an icon brief, to make sure that the requirements are understood and necessary.

What is it for?

Is it warning the user that something different will happen, such as playing a video instead of opening a larger version of an image? Is it for wayfinding — directing the user to go somewhere?

What is its context?

Is it used on a toolbar, alongside a text link or displayed small in a list? For example, if they're for a website or application, there may be designs, or at least wireframes, that will give you a sense of where the icons will be used, what size they will need to be and their proximity to each other. Sometimes, the space available for an icon means that it will be too small to be of any use.

Who's it for?

Is there an age, gender or cultural focus that needs to be considered? The icon you would create for a primary school e-learning tool would be different to one aimed at an older audience. Just as you might use personas and stories to decide how to structure a website, you can treat the icons in a similar way.

Is there a single message?

Sometimes a brief tries to convey too much information with a single icon (history of customer support requests), when focusing on one aspect would be more effective (history).

Does it need to be an icon?

Could it work just as well without it? Does it solve language problems or help with a lack of space? Would using only text make it harder to discover at a glance? Does it need accompanying text to make it understandable? A site for an application may want to drive visitors to download the software and try it out for themselves, in which case combining the link with a down arrow icon would increase its visibility. It may not be worthwhile creating an icon for every navigation item, though, like links to terms of service or other legal documentation.

   After discussing these criteria, any unnecessary icons have been pruned (and perhaps new icons added to the list), and their context and purpose are understood.

Finding the metaphor

We can now begin the first part of the design process: deciding on the correct metaphor to use. The first consideration should always be whether there is an existing convention or standard. Familiarity makes an icon functional and recognisable, but the process of discovering an existing standard ranges from easy to the nigh-on impossible. Some, like a house to communicate *home*, a clock to convey *history*, or a piece of paper with a folded corner for *document* you will know without having to think about it. Others, like *view*, may not be immediately obvious. Thankfully, there are some useful resources out there to help you check whether a convention exists.

Google image search

http://images.google.com/

It's obvious but definitely worth mentioning. The first stop is always a Google image search as its breadth of results is unparalleled. There is even a filter option in the sidebar to narrow the search results down to icons, but don't just use that. Sometimes a metaphor can be found from photographs and illustrations as much as existing icons.

The Noun Project

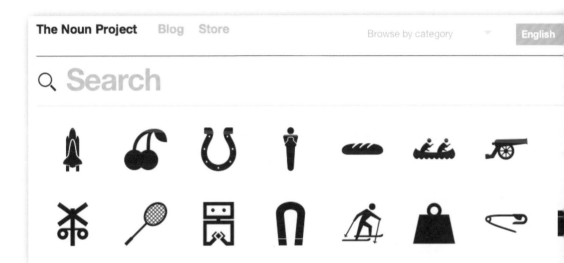

http://thenounproject.com

With a mission of "sharing, celebrating and enhancing the world's visual language", the Noun Project is an ever-growing online resource, collating metaphors for various categories such as transportation and healthcare. It doesn't aim to present a single image for each noun though: rather, it collects as many different interpretations as it can find.

The Noun Project's collection of bicycle symbols

Iconfinder.com

http://www.iconfinder.com/

A search engine, specifically created for icons. Again, this will show you any possible interpretation and allow you to search by size. Restricting the size of the results will filter out more illustrative application icons, leaving you with the more useful symbols.

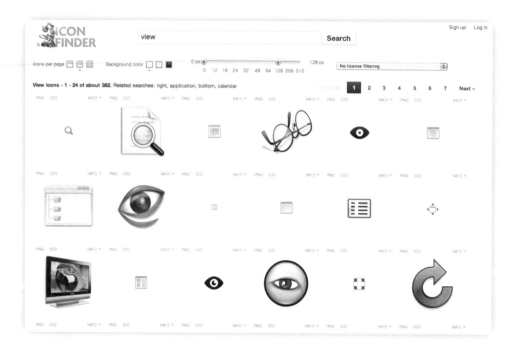

Just as important, there is a lot of value in ad hoc testing on people. A typical question I ask in our studio is, "If I said to you 'submit a support request', what image do you think of?". The first images that come to people's minds can often be useful.

Interview

Stephen Horlander's RSS icon

A lot of the metaphors we use today have been in existence for a long time. The pictogram for information point, for example, was in use before I was born, so I can't remember a time when that convention didn't exist.

The rapid technical progress of the web has brought with it a need for a whole new set of metaphors. Prior to 2004, a wide variety of esoteric symbols were used to depict an RSS feed, from (bizarrely) medication to coffee cups. The most common was the simple orange block with 'RSS', as seen above in Firefox 0.9.

The problem with using the text RSS was that, technically, it's just one format a feed could be in. It was shorter than 'Syndication' at least. A way of describing the concept, rather than one particular implementation, was needed. Up to this point, it was still better than a pill or coffee cup, though. That all changed very quickly, when Stephen Horlander created a new RSS icon for Firefox 1.0.

The white radio waves indicate the broadcasting aspect of feeds clearly and simply. By 2005, however, Microsoft's Internet Explorer and Outlook had adopted it too, followed by Opera the following year. Microsoft's decision was the catalyst it needed and it was quickly established as a recognised standard.

Standardisation is very important with icons. Choosing to go against an existing standard means you lose the advantage of familiarity, risk confusion, or not being noticed at all. That's why site owners will now use the RSS icon standard, rather than an obscure metaphor such as the pill.

Were there any elements of other prior attempts at a feed icon that were useful to you? Were you starting from scratch?

" *There were not very many examples of attempts at a universal feed icon existing at the time. Most websites were using a sprawling list of buttons labelled with various syndication formats, which was one of the main problems we were hoping to solve.*

How did you arrive at the final icon? Were there many sketches and iterations before that point?

" *A lightning bolt was the original icon being used to represent feeds in Firefox at the time. I did several sketches trying to incorporate that, but it didn't really seem to be working. They were too complicated and didn't really seem to convey the right message. We finally settled on the idea of waves originating and emanating from a source. I ran with that idea and turned it into the version of the feed icon that ultimately shipped.*

Did you have any idea that the icon you designed would become the international standard? How does it feel now that it is?

" *At the time I had no idea that it would take off like it has. The principle behind the design was to create a single simple icon that could be used to unify and represent all syndication protocols. Which is almost exactly what happened. It is one of those rare instances where the result you hope to achieve matches almost perfectly with what you actually achieve. We put the icon out there and people just picked it up and adopted it. It spawned T-shirts and websites and really got people behind it. It feels pretty amazing to be a part of something like that.*

Stephen Horlander's original ideas for the RSS icon

In a similar vein, there are a number of 'open icon' projects, where the community is attempting to establish a standard and repeat the success of the RSS icon:

- Sharing - *http://www.shareaholic.com/openshareicon*
- Language - *http://www.languageicon.org/*
- OPML - *http://www.opmlicons.com/*
- Geotag - *http://www.geotagicons.com/*

All of these have been made with a Creative Commons licence to aid their adoption. One in particular, the Open Share Icon, has been adopted by Microsoft for their new Metro UI and, as such, is set to become a standard very soon.

But how closely do we need to stick to a standard? Surely there's room for some individuality? An online study undertaken by Iconglobe.net, a "comparative test of public symbols" tested existing public symbols and pictogram standards. Interviewees were asked to choose the most easily identifiable sign out of four variants in each topic. Each of the variants was a real example found in the wild.

The results demonstrated how much variations in the recognised symbol made the symbols less recognisable. In this case, the information symbol:

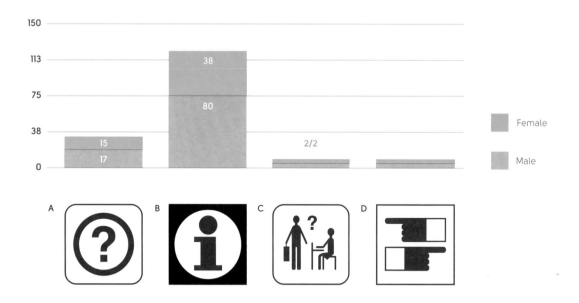

The information icon in C is open to a lot of different interpretations. Is that a briefcase or a bat in the standing person's hand? Is that the hem of a skirt dangling beneath the chair of the seated figure, or something altogether ruder? The negative effects of fiddling with an established standard are clear. Without a familiar configuration, icons can take longer to decipher or, at worst, confuse completely: the opposite of their purpose. If there is a standard, use it to give your icon the best chance of being understood quickly.

However, like life, it's not so black and white. There are occasions when you might need to stray from the standard, such as:

- Just because an icon is a standard, it may not have open usage rights or copyright may not be clear. For example, many of the icons Apple creates are recognisable metaphors but are also trademarked. Recently, the icon originally developed by the web community for share was bought by a company, who then changed its licence terms.

- There could be potential confusion with another icon in the set. For example, a magnifying glass is used for both search and zoom. The latter often has a plus sign added for clarity, but that may not be enough.

- There could be a negative or opposite connotation in the culture of the intended audience. Remember how in Chapter 2 the metaphor of an owl had two meanings — wisdom (in the West) and stupidity (in Asia).

While some icons do have an existing standard, their days are surely numbered. A great example of this is the 3½-inch floppy disk, which is still the most used metaphor for *save file*. For how long will this last? Not only have floppies become obsolete, but they weren't around for very long in the first place. Generations are growing up with no experience or knowledge of them. Consider other icons that use objects, such as the classic diamond shape envelope. This is an object that has been in constant use since the nineteenth century and shows no signs of being phased out quite yet. It's still a robust and familiar metaphor for email.

While some pictograms may become less useful over time as the objects they represent fade from use, others could take on a life of their own and become arbitrary. It's possible that in the future, the map pin origins of the geolocation icon will become forgotten — it will simply be recognised as an arbitrary symbol.

Starting from scratch

If, after all your research, no existing standard can be found, or there are problems with using the standard, then you have to start the process of creating your own! In the case of our *view* icon, there are no existing conventions, except for the magnifying glass. In the context of a browser UI, this would be too close to search.

This part can seem daunting, especially as you won't have any prior use to aid recognition, but it can still be successful. The creative challenge of creating your own metaphor makes it all the more satisfying than simply reproducing another *home* icon. Even if an icon isn't immediately obvious, if it can intrigue the viewer or make an impression, that can be enough to make it work.

In general, the golden rule is to steer clear of using any text, such as the first letter, for the simple reason that it won't translate into other languages. As always, there are exceptions to this rule, such as the widely used information sign, and if it works with the language of the intended audience, then it can be a possibility. For similar localisation problems, it's worth avoiding depictions of body parts. Thumbs up may generally be a positive sign, but in Iran it's considered an obscene gesture. Again, it depends on the context.

It's better to consider more universally understandable options first, and I find the best way to kickstart the thinking process for a new icon metaphor is drawing a mind map. There's often more than one way of representing something, and a mind map is a way of exploring that.

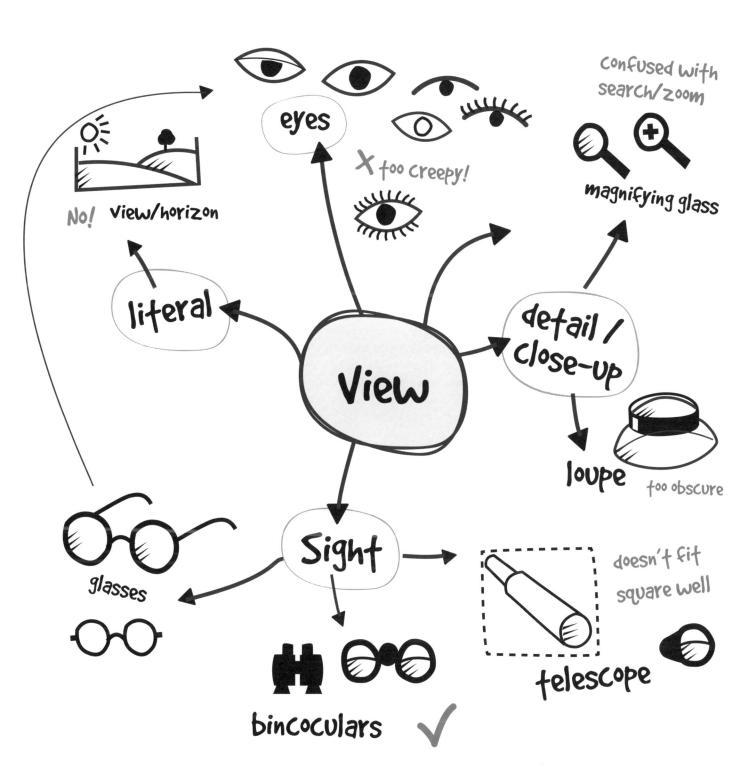

Starting with the icon name in the centre, write down anything that comes to mind, no matter how abstract or seemingly worthless at the time. Keep the related ideas on the same branch, with different tangents going off on new branches. At each node, sketch out the ideas as you go — there can be more than one way to visualise an object.

If you're struggling to find a good metaphor, is there a fun angle that can be explored? Humour, when judged correctly, can entice a user to spend time finding out what a symbol means, as well as making it memorable. In this example, the Harry Potter glasses might be fun and distinctive but not particularly effective in communicating *view*.

The binoculars metaphor feels like the strongest of these ideas and there are a few criteria to help you check whether you've found the right metaphor:

- **If it's a pictogram, is it recognisable?** How easily can it be misconstrued as something else? A silhouette of a heavy weight could also look like handbag.

Classic examples of this are the instructional symbols used on hand dryers that appear to dispense bacon at the push of a button:

Push button   **Receive bacon**   **Applaud the jellyfish**

Sometimes there may be supporting text which can help reinforce the meaning, though.

- **How much detail is required to make it recognisable?** Can it be adequately rendered in the space available? A padlock can still be recognisable at 8px, but a train doesn't stand a chance.

- **Are there any negative connotations?** Specifically, cultural problems with the intended audience?

Even once this was chosen, there was a variety of perspectives and styles that could be considered.

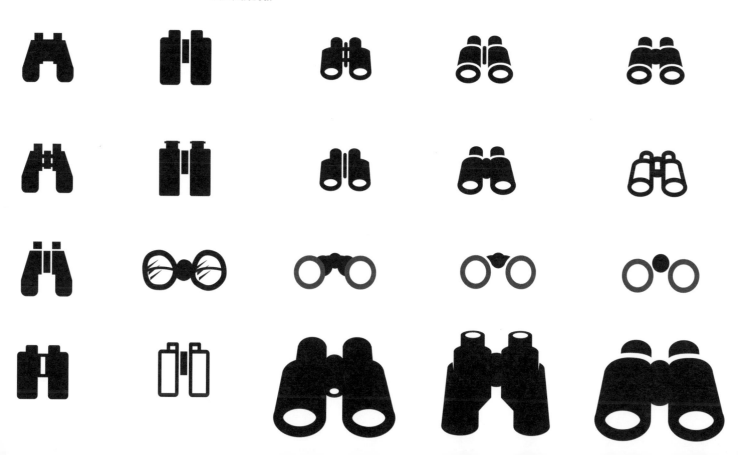

The binoculars metaphor was the best solution for the context because:

- It had a unique profile, reducing confusion with other icons in the UI.
- It was a familiar object that could be rendered effectively without looking like other things.
- There were no negative connotations.
- Most importantly, it communicated *view* without too many alternative meanings.

The solution in this instance was a pictogram, but sometimes it might have to be an ideogram or something more abstract or arbitrary.

Many companies are now having to find a metaphor for *applications*. Apple has created a memorable icon for this, in the shape of a brush, ruler and pen, forming a letter A.

While using the first letter is usually avoided, app has more international usage as a word and, more importantly, the icon doesn't depend on knowledge of that in order to work. All very nice but, while recognisable, it's a trademark rather than an open standard and therefore can't be used. This means research into how others represent *apps*. Boxee, the social media centre software, came up with an elegant solution for its UI, with a very abstract shape for *apps*:

Using combinations

If the brief specifies icons with similar functions, consider a modular system that combines other icons or shapes in order to create the metaphor.

As an example, a document might have three variants: Add, Private and Locked. Starting with the icon of the base element — the document icon with folded corner — smaller icons (badges) are then added to convey the different states:

Notice how they don't line up with the base icon? This simple visual change helps draw attention to the added meaning, which in turn helps separate a series of very similar icons. The bottom-right area of the document icon is a good place for these, as it naturally has white space in that portion. Top-right would obscure a crucial part of the icon, making it simply a rectangle. If final size permits, it could work equally well inside the shape:

Thinking back to Neurath's Isotype system, another approach could be to combine the base icon with a meaningful outline, such as the warning triangle.

On its own, the symbol can simply mean power or electricity source. Adding the triangle makes it clear that in this context it's a warning. This has the disadvantage, however, of reducing the size of the base icon.

Or a shape can be overlaid on the base icon in a similar way. This microphone icon needs a state to show when sound has been muted — which can be achieved by using a diagonal line to cross out the base icon. This can work well, as long as the line doesn't obscure the base icon to the extent that it becomes unrecognisable.

The appendix contains a chart of the common badges you can use to provide additional meaning.

Using colour

The final part of the metaphor is the use of colour. While colour alone can't be relied upon to convey a message, it can help reinforce the icon's message or change its visual importance compared with others. It's often the first thing to grab our attention.

Used in isolation, colour can provide feedback, confirming success or warning of errors, but not always reliably. Everyone interprets colour differently and while for most that difference is tiny, one in twelve people have some sort of colour vision deficiency*. I'm one of them, and my colour-blindness can cause problems. Think of those little lights on devices like network routers that change from green to red to show when there's a problem. I can't tell them apart, partly because they're so small. It's easier to see a change in the colour when it's used on a larger area.

There are also potential issues with cultural differences again. While black can represent mourning, fear or even evil, it can also convey sophistication and luxury. Opposite are some example colour comparisons, with their positive and negative implications, along with more modern, technical associations.

The key is not to use colour alone to convey the message, but to use it in conjunction with other identifiers. Going back to our document icon with its three different states, we can add colour to reinforce their meaning.

Temperature	Colour	Positive	Negative	Technical
Warm	Red	Importance, warmth, life (blood), love, revolution, celebration and good luck (China)	Stop, problems, danger	Warning, error
	Orange	Warmth, energy	Cheap	RSS
	Yellow	Joy, happiness, light, wisdom	Warning (combined with black), forbidden, cowardice, decay	Secure, highlight
Warm/cool mix	Green	Life, nature, vitality, go, growth	Envy, madness	Sharing, correct
	Purple	Royalty	Cruelty, arrogance	
Cool	Blue	Daytime, calm, information, corporate	Cold, corporate	Selected, on, enabled
	Grey	Luxury	Sadness	Disabled, off
Neutral	Brown	Comfort, nature	Poverty	
	Black	Sophistication, luxury, expensive, prosperity	Death, mourning, evil, mystery, misery	

The exception to the rule

As this book covers a wide range of icon types there is, of course, a category that doesn't quite fit the approach discussed in this chapter: application icons. Chapter 7 covers these and the areas in which the metaphor process differs.

Summary

Always research whether an icon has an existing convention first. Unless there are potential problems with trademarks, negative connotations or confusion with other icons in the set, it makes sense to use the convention. However, if there isn't, have fun working out your own metaphor. It needn't be immediately obvious, but it does need to be understandable. Whatever you choose, the context is everything.

Chapter references

Susan Kare interview
http://www-sul.stanford.edu/mac/primary/interviews/kare/books.html

Comparative test of public symbols
http://www.iconglobe.net/blog/2007/05/06/comparative-test-of-public-symbols-test-results/

The open share icon
http://blog.shareaholic.com/2009/05/the-open-share-icon-100-open-community-driven-goodness/

Colour-blindness statistics
*http://www.iamcal.com/toys/colors/stats.php

Further reading

Usability in icons
http://stiern.com/articles/usability/usability-in-icons/
Particularly looking at the traditional 'link' icon and its clarity outside of geek circles iconathon

Iconathon
http://iconathon.org/
The Iconathon is an initiative run by Code for America, in partnership with the Noun Project, to collaboratively design new civic symbols for the public domain.
The events are fun and creative events that let you give back to your cities.

Chapter 5

Drawing icons

At this point in the book, we've been through the initial process of reading the brief, checking for existing conventions, and deciding on the right metaphor to use. We've also created some simple favicons — now let's move on to creating some proper icons! In this chapter we'll look at the drawing process, then in Chapter 6 we'll consider the final file format and deployment method for the icon which can have a bearing on how we create the artwork. We'll start with simple pictograms and then move on to small colour icons.

We've already covered some basics of drawing to crisp pixels in Chapter 3 about favicons. This chapter will build further on that, introducing the concepts of balance and consistency.

Rules for drawing

"The first rule is ... there are no rules!"

Goku, Dragonball Z

Drawing style is as personal as the tool you use to draw, and not everyone will use the same methods, even if the end result looks the same.

The intention of this chapter isn't to lay down any rules, but instead to offer guidelines and possible ways of working, as well as show how various designers approach their work. Even though I have my set ways of working, I've definitely adopted some of the techniques gleaned from talking to other designers.

Having said all that, there are two particular rules that I stick to, especially when creating a suite of icons for an interface: it makes sense to create them in context and in company.

In context

If the icons need to sit on top of other elements, such as on a toolbar with a gradient, incorporate this into your artwork. If it needs to work on top of multiple colours, or be positioned on top of busy or unpredictable backgrounds such as a photo, include those too. Place these contexts on separate layers that can be hidden before export. Don't wait until the icon is in use to discover that it doesn't work unless it's on a white background all by itself.

In company

When creating an icon set, don't create a new document for each icon, where it's viewed in isolation, if you can help it. Set them up together and use either multiple artboards (Illustrator CS4+), pages and states (Fireworks) or slices (Photoshop and many others) to export them as individual files. This helps to avoid inconsistency in the artwork, be it in size, colour, weight or style. If you're designing a set of icons intended for a sidebar of a UI, draw the icons together on that sidebar.

When I created this icon set for the Jolicloud interface, each was placed on its own artboard, and I included the dark toolbar background on a separate layer that was hidden before export

Sometimes, the context demands that all icons are together in one file. For example, when working on toolbar icons for Windows, you can provide an ICO for each one, but it is far easier to provide them all together in an image strip which can contain multiple sizes where required:

A Windows toolbar image strip, containing the two sizes

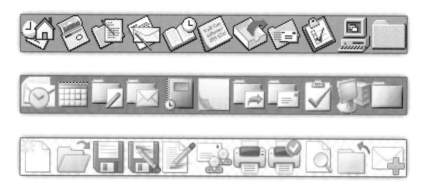

If you use CSS sprites to deploy your icons on a website (more about this method in Chapter 6), then you will also need to create your icons together.

With Adobe Illustrator's multiple artboards, it's possible to create many versions of an icon and keep the rejected ones within the document, but outside the artboard or canvas area. Only the artwork on the artboard is exported (the exception being SVG, which will include all the surplus artwork). Save it in another document if you have to, but never throw anything away — it's all potentially useful at some point.

Tools

The first tool you need is almost so obvious that it shouldn't need mentioning, but I will anyway for completeness: paper and 'something to make a mark' (as my life drawing teacher put it). I've only recently realised that graph paper notebooks make excellent icon sketching pads, especially those with light, subtle lines. You can just use the backs of envelopes and a free biro from a bank, though: if it lets you sketch and try out ideas quickly, then it works.

As I've mentioned before, this book doesn't presume what graphics editor you use — tools are personal, and what's right for me may not be for you. However, as we move into drawing pictograms, there are some features that you should look out for that will aid the process:

- **Vector drawing**
While there might be bitmap effects and fine-tuning applied as raster artwork, the basis of the icon should be vector. This will make editing easy and it provides a basis for creating other sizes as well as high resolution for print, should they be needed.

- **Pixel grid**
Much of the drawing process of icons intended for screen use will involve placing the nodes of vector paths either on or (deliberately) between pixels. An accurate grid will let you see where you're going. Adobe Illustrator handily enables a pixel grid when zoomed in to the artwork at 600% or more, keeping it out of the way until you need it.

- **Pixel preview**
This sounds obvious, but not every vector drawing app will actually let you see your work as pixels — Lineform is such a program. As a consequence, you only see it once the artwork is exported, which is too late.

ICON HANDBOOK- SECTION ICONS

Echos susan Kare.

Meccanno?

Application Icons

Favicons!

- **Export options**
As a minimum you should be able to export as PNG, but the ability to save as SVG, PDF and EPS is very useful too. Opacity and Sketch currently support the largest range of export formats.

The appendix lists the major applications you are likely to use, as well as those from smaller independent developers, and highlights some of their pros and cons.

Sizing

Size is the first factor to affect the artwork, and when creating small monochrome icons, every pixel counts. The smaller it is, the less detail you can use to get the message across.

Normally, icons are square, sized in even numbers of pixels and multiples — 16px, 32px, 48px, and so on, being the most common. The context will often determine this; for example, a tab bar icon for the iPhone 4 would require a 60×60px icon, while its document icon would be 44×58px (see, not always square!). The appendix contains a comprehensive reference chart (or see online at *http://iconhandbook.co.uk/reference/chart/*) that will help here, detailing what sizes and formats you'll need for popular contexts, and even listing naming conventions where necessary.

If there are no specifications for the intended context then it's up to you, and there are occasions when an odd-numbered grid suits the artwork best.

 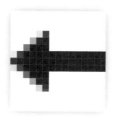

In this 16×16px example, an arrow is drawn on an even grid, and the point falls exactly on the gridline.

However, owing to the way anti-aliasing works, two pixels are rendered for the point, which makes it look blunt or rounded.

Compare it with the same arrow on an odd-numbered grid at 15×15px. Here, the point falls in the centre of a pixel, so it only uses one pixel and the point no longer looks blunt. If you wanted the arrow to have a slightly rounded appearance, then the bluntness would be the right choice, of course — both approaches have advantages in different contexts. An odd-numbered grid would also give you different weight options, and enable the icon to be centred within a circle.

Text size may also affect the size of the icons. If they're intended to work next to a text label, you may want to specify a size that works for both. This doesn't necessarily mean that it should be exactly the same size: it may make the icon too small. See how Dribbble's icons (above) are just a few pixels larger. This gives enough space to make the icon clear, but not so much that it is obviously larger — the balance is perfect!

Drawing for balance and consistency

Once you know your icon size, it's very tempting to fill the entire area with the icon, so it takes up as much of the space as it can. But to enable the viewer to easily distinguish each icon, they need to have a different outline, which in turn will have a different visual size. This will become obvious when you draw icons in company. In this example, the heart and star in particular look small in comparison with the square.

Of all these shapes, the square needs to be the smallest. If the canvas size is 32px, sticking to a rough guideline of making a square 75–80% (whichever gives a even number) of the original size will make it 24px, and give us an inner margin of 4px (32×0.75=24 and 32−24÷2=4). The circle then overlaps this guide, while irregular shapes like the star and heart are allowed to take the entire space, and the cross is somewhere in between. In the same way, the diagonal bar needs to be shorter than a vertical or horizontal one, such as those in the plus sign:

Now they look balanced. This is why it's important to design icons in company as well as context — the imbalance would be hard to spot when dealing with each icon as a separate file. The binoculars icon metaphor for view that we looked at in Chapter 4 will be an irregular shape and, therefore, needs to take up most of the space.

A consistent style also helps balance your icons. Where possible, keep stroke widths consistent and avoid clashing styles:

Consistency isn't a function of a strict numerical value, unfortunately, as optical illusions skew our perceptions. Because of anti-aliasing, a 2px line will appear thicker at 45° than when it's horizontal. This happens to corners of rounded rectangles as well. In these instances, you need to tweak them by eye. If your 1px stroke looks too heavy, try reducing it to 0.9px. This is often enough to trim off some stray subpixels and make it appear lighter. In general, you will have to trust your eye, but these suggestions should be a handy guide, and help you know what to look out for.

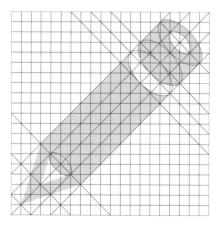

Traditional pictogram design would normally use a grid to help ensure consistency across the complete set, and when creating icons for screen use, we already have the pixel grid. The sizes involved often mean that anything more complex would be unnecessary, but if the icons need to be larger, you might find one useful. As with all grids, though, they are simply a guide.

Consistency is important, but breaking it can be a useful trick to pull — for example, when you want to grab attention. Flickr uses very small and simple icons for its navigation and photo actions, but when it really wants you to notice something, such as the confirmation that a photo has been deleted, the style changes:

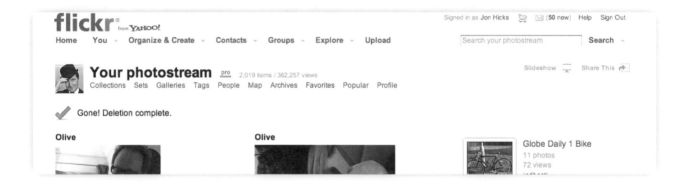

Drawing for scaling

Different contexts and resolutions will demand different size versions of the same icon, or at least planning to ensure correct scaling. Usually, where an icon requires different sizes, they're neat multiples of each other — 16px, 32px, 64px, and so on. There are no hard and fast rules for where you should start, although many designers prefer to create the largest first and then scale down, just as we did with favicons in Chapter 3.

In the following example, an icon used on a web app needs two versions: one for standard resolutions and a higher resolution version for use on the iPhone 4 Retina display, where the icon needs to be the same resolution (72 dpi) but twice the size. Keeping the multiplication in mind, a 1px stroke on the 32px icon will need to be 2px on the 64px version.

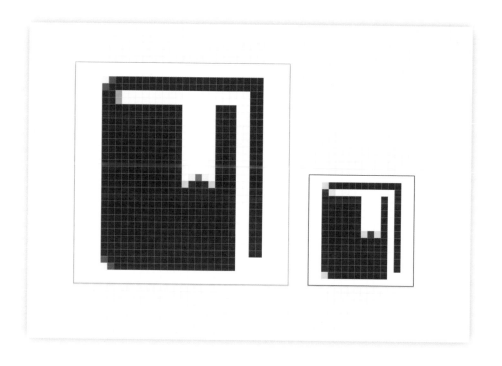

When implemented, the double-sized icon will then look right (and high quality to boot!). Not all multiple size icons are for supporting multiple resolutions, however. It may be that the larger icon is just shown in a different context. For example, Mac OS X toolbars have two size settings. By default, the toolbar will consist of 32px icons, but if the option to use a smaller size is chosen, it will display 24px versions.

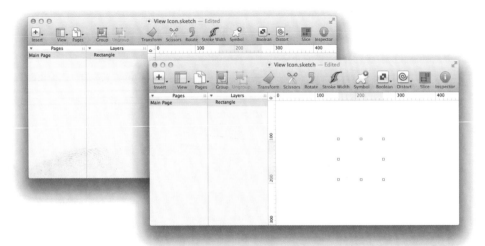

The toolbar in Sketch has pixel-perfect versions for both normal and small sizes, chosen via a context menu

Here it wouldn't make sense to scale elements like strokes, as you would always want them to be displayed at the same weight. It depends on the context and the size, so it's important to have them established before you start drawing so that you can plan ahead.

Other than simply resizing artwork, it would be nice if there was a way of avoiding altogether the laborious task of creating each size. Normally this isn't possible, but there are some strategies that might help:

• Using Photoshop's smart objects or Illustrator's symbols, you could create a common base icon and scale this up, adding progressively more detail as necessary to the larger sizes. Illustrator's snap to pixels command can help with some basic optimisation.

• Opacity was created to deal with the task of drawing multiple resolutions. If you keep detail on a separate layer, it can then be shown or hidden via the app's variables feature at certain resolutions.

While these techniques can help in some situations, it's fair to say that you're still going to be spending time tweaking each scaled piece of artwork individually, to get the optimisation just right!

Tip: if you're enlarging or reducing icons in Illustrator, it doesn't always resize artwork precisely. To keep coordinates and dimensions as round numbers, draw a path with an empty fill, and stroke behind the artwork to the artboard bounds. Then, when you resize, it gives Illustrator a neat frame to guide it.

How much detail to include?

It's obvious that icons need to be simple: the more detail you add, the longer it takes for the brain to decode it. The reverse is also true, as some icons require a certain level of detail in order to be recognisable.

For example, the concept of history is normally shown as a clock face. This translates very well to an extremely simplified form. Compared with a detailed version of the same metaphor, the simple icon is undoubtedly clearer:

On the other hand, the iPhone icon below (left) has been drawn in its simplest form. At this level, it could be anything from a picture frame to an Amazon Kindle, and needs the details of the speaker and home button to make it clear (below right):

Other than excessive detail, there are other mistakes that reduce an icon's clarity:

- Excessive shadows and borders
- Too much anti-aliasing (often due to perspective — see later on in this chapter)
- Straight pixels not crisp

If you're making multiple sizes, larger icons would normally show more detail, but this is more a question of style, and a minimalist look (such as the icons on Vimeo) might be preferable.

Suggesting form

Even in monochrome, it's possible to convey the form of an object. Consider how light falls on something and where its darker edges would be. Using line thickness, top edges where light catches the object and areas where there is no depth can be depicted with thin strokes, while the sides and bottoms of objects where there is depth can warrant a thicker stroke.

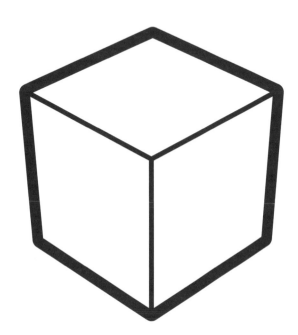

With this idea in mind, a piece of paper on a flat surface would have the same line thickness all around, whereas an isometric cube could have double line thickness on each edge except the three closest to you. Altering the tone of the stroke can also have this effect — lighter shades make the area feel closer.

Where a shadow is cast, the negative space can be used to suggest it. Likewise, any highlighted area can encroach into the negative space, as long as it doesn't obscure the shape:

Negative space can also be used to avoid overcomplicating the artwork such as the handle on this bucket icon from Dribbble.

By showing the shadow of the handle on the outside of the bucket, the impression is one of a complete handle. Our brains fill in the gaps.

Drawing with perspective

The smaller your icon is, the less useful depth and perspective become. Icons of 32px or smaller benefit from being viewed face-on, as perspective not only reduces the physical size of the image, it also introduces more anti-aliased edges that reduce the clarity of the artwork:

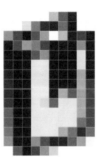

Nevertheless, it's still possible, and sometimes essential, to show foreshortening (where the depth of an object depicts the illusion of getting smaller the further away it is) without using an isometric view. The first example is a representation of an inbox:

While this is a standard metaphor, especially in email clients, the icon only works with some perspective. Viewed from the front or top it isn't really recognisable at all, but by keeping the front flat and extending the object at the back, it's clear what it is. It's also possible to suggest depth without using any foreshortening at all, such as with these wallet and book icons:

Again, without the suggestion of depth it would be less apparent what the icons represent.

Reusing characters from fonts

Sometimes the symbol you need may exist in, or possibly use elements from, an existing font. For example, when creating an icon for help, the convention of the question mark should mean using a font is a good move, and it can be. As with all icons, the smaller it is, the more likely you'll need to re-create it from scratch to ensure clarity. When working on icons 16px or smaller, it's worth trying a font that has been specifically designed to work on screen at a small size, such as Verdana.

Here is a comparison of the question mark using Helvetica Bold, at 32px and then 16px. At 12px, you can see the difference between Helvetica (left) and Verdana (right).

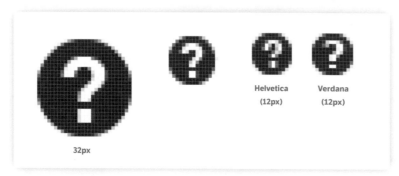

At these small sizes, it's particularly helpful to have pixel fonts (also called bitmap fonts) like Mini and Cellular installed. While these may seem like a relic of a past creating Flash sites, they are already optimised to aliasing at small sizes, and each font still has room for variety:

Furthermore, your graphics editor may allow control over the anti-aliasing of the font, as well as the ability to specify text sizes with decimal places, in order to get the best out of each glyph. If, after tweaking these settings, you still can't get a crisp symbol, the rendered font can be used as a guide, but will look better re-created from pixels in the same way we did in Chapter 3 on favicons.

Draw, pardner! Getting practical

So, let's take all of the ideas we've covered so far and put them into practice. I've chosen the book icon from page 128; we'll create it in 32px and 16px sizes for use on a website. The final format is most likely going to be PNG, so it won't require any special consideration other than being pixel crisp.

There are, of course, many different ways you could draw this, and no right way, but this is my approach. I'm going to use Illustrator, but most of the terms covered should apply to other applications too. We'll use w, h, x and y as shorthand for width, height, x-position and y-position respectively, measured from the top left corner of the canvas.

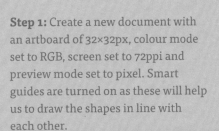

Step 1: Create a new document with an artboard of 32×32px, colour mode set to RGB, screen set to 72ppi and preview mode set to pixel. Smart guides are turned on as these will help us to draw the shapes in line with each other.

    As we've chosen 32px as the icon size, the subject is rectangular and we want it to scale neatly by half to 16px, We'll leave an even 2px margin (rather than 3px). It won't reach this far left and right, as the book shape isn't square, but it will touch the top and bottom margins.

Step 2: Start by drawing a plain black rectangle (w:17px; h:24px; x:7px; y:6px).

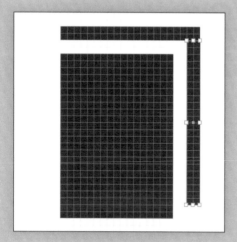 

Step 3: Then draw the back cover, consisting of two vector rectangles. As the size is 32px, these lines should be 2px wide so we'll leave the same amount of space to represent the pages of the book. We can, of course, use a 2px stroke to create these lines but rectangles are generally quicker and easier. It means not having to faff about with the position of the stroke (centre, outside or inside) — it lands exactly where we want it to.

Draw the top part (w:21px; h:2px; x:7px; y:2px) and the right-hand edge (w:2px; h:24px; x:26px; y:4px).

Step 4: Next, we want to suggest the curve of the spine on the left-hand side, so we'll draw a circle at the top to create the radius (w:6px; h:6px; x:4px; y:2px), then drag-copy this to the bottom (x:4px; y:24px).

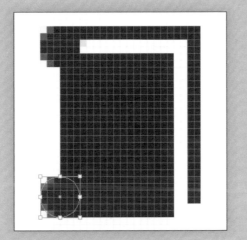
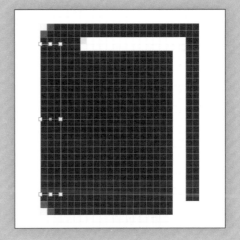

Step 5: Then, draw another rectangle to fill in the gap between these two circles, going from the centre of the top circle, to the centre of the bottom one (w:4px; h:22px; x:4px; y:5px).

Step 6: Returning to the top circle, we'll copy it and paste it in front (the sequence ⌘C ⌘F in Illustrator is second nature to me these days!), which puts it right on top of the first one, rather than offsetting it. We then want to reduce it by 2px. Holding down the Alt key when resizing it anchors the scaling to the centre. This is then filled with white. (If you find it easier to simply draw a new circle, it's: w:2px; h:2px; x:6px; y:4px.) In pixel preview, you'll notice that this looks like a 2×2px grey square, but if you switch to normal view mode (called overprint in Illustrator), you'll see the circle. While we could have drawn a square and reduced its opacity to get the same effect, we want to make sure this artwork can be reused larger in the future.

Step 7: Next, draw a white rectangle to temporarily mask the part of the black circle on the right that we don't want (w:4px; h:2px; x:7px; y:4px). We'll make this more permanent later.

Step 8: To create the bookmark, we'll start with a white rectangle (w:5px; h:12px; x:16px; y:6px).

We'll then add a new anchor point on the bottom edge in the centre, select just this point, then move it up 2px. If snap to pixels is on, this will need to be turned off, as we need the anchor point to sit between two pixels. We'll specifically choose a 5px wide bookmark to give a clear centre point (look back to the arrow example at the start of this chapter).

Compared with the 4px version, 5px looks much sharper.

This means that it won't scale down as neatly to 16px as the other shapes we've drawn, so this will need to be tweaked. It's worth it, though!

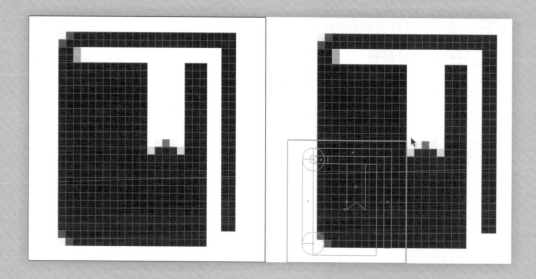

Step 9: Before we clean this one up, we'll create the 16px version, so add a new 16×16px art board to the document. As mentioned earlier, I find that Illustrator scales artwork better when given a neat boundary, so draw a 32×32px square on the first artboard, make sure it has neither fill nor stroke, and then drag-copy all the art across to the 16px artboard, with the transparent square defining the artwork bounds. We can then either use the scale tool to resize it by 50% or simply shift-drag a corner until it snaps with the new artboard.

As predicted, the bookmark needed tweaking to fit, but that only takes a second.

Now that the icon is drawn, we just need to clean up the white shapes used to temporarily mask areas. We can do this using pathfinder tools (sometimes called boolean operations in other apps) to subtract the white shapes from the black ones behind. Then we can join all the shapes together into one. If you didn't want the white areas to be transparent, you would, of course, be able to skip all this cleaning up!

Sometimes, there will be just a little more tweaking to be done. This means using the remove anchor point tool (- key) to get rid of some unwanted anchor points left over from this process. Subtracting also means the anchor points may have to be tweaked to get them right. In the case of the bookmark, it's lost some of the definition from the points, so these are pulled down slightly.

Again, snap to pixels will need to be disabled to do this. Now that our monochrome bookmark icon is done, we can style it how we want: perhaps a 1px drop-shadow of 20% opacity white to give it the look of being embedded; or an inner stroke. We also have an icon that works for contexts other than screen, too, such as in a printed book like this one!

Drawn icon set

So far, we've seen icons in a very straight, clean-cut style, keeping to pixel grids, and ensuring crisp edges. There's still room for style and expression though, and a great example of this is Fred LeBlanc's Drawn icon set.

Fred has managed to retain clarity as well as the scalability of vectors while creating an icon set that is warm and unique. I quizzed Fred about his workflow and approach to making his Drawn icon set.

DRAWN

◆ SET ONE ◆

http://fredhq.com/shop/drawn

OUTLINES

Step 1: What icons do I make?

This has really been the hardest part so far — both in set one, and while working on set two where it's getting harder after each icon is made. Generally I've been asking friends what icons they'd find useful and creating lists from there.

Being a rather big fan of icons myself, I have a number of sets, so looking through those for common themes also helps. There are some icons that people expect to get, but I didn't want a normal set, so I made sure that I'd hit 50% of the normal icons you find, with the other 50% being a mixed bag of whatever I could think of.

I was a boy scout, so I made a tent, square knot and campfire. We're expecting our first child on Halloween, so I made a couple of baby icons [author's note: Fred's daughter Amelia Rose was born on 19 October 2011 — congratulations!]. I just cancelled my subscription to ManPacks, which is where the clothing icons came from. We recently had a rare tornado freak out in our area, thus the weather icons.

Inspiration has come from wherever I can find it.

Step 2: Making 'em

Next, there are two ways that I'll create an icon depending on how confident I am. One: I'll just grab the pen tool and have at it. I draw the outline of the icon with my pen settings set to black stroke, white background, 2px weight, round cap and round join. Once I have the initial shape, I tweak things a bit. I've been getting better with the pen tool, but I'm no where near mastery of it.

Next, I shrink down the stroke size to 1px (same round cap and round join) and add detail lines. At this point, I'm just adding all of the other lines that'll make the outline represent what the shape is supposed to be. Sometimes I get carried away (the rocking-horse might be an example of that). Other times it's very limited (the funnel icon shows that). I try to use as few lines as possible, but still make the icons unique and easily recognisable, which varies depending on how much people expect to see a certain icon.

The other method is by doing some Google image searching. I did a bit of this process in my lawnmower icon on Dribbble:

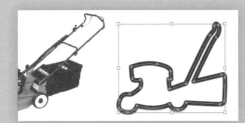  

Starting out: *http://drbl.in/brfv*

What I thought was finished:
http://drbl.in/brfF

The one that shipped:
http://cl.ly/2a3j1e3n171l2r1M3C0Z

I don't sketch and I don't trace. I might as well trace, because I might sit at one icon for an hour looking left at the image and right at my icon until it's right, but I make it a point not to trace (for both copyright and artistic reasons).

Lastly, for creating the shape, some icons have areas that have no stroke and a black background. The USB symbol on the thumb drive icon and the inside of the tornado icon are examples of this.

Step 3: Converting to shapes

While still in line form, I scaled each icon to fit inside a 48×48px box. Some icons are drawn rather large and then shrunk down; some are drawn at actual size. Honestly, I just start drawing and adjust at the end of each icon. I have three actions created that do this:

- Object → Path → Outline stroke
- Effect → Pathfinder: merge
- Scale to a 48×48px box

Icons whose longest dimension is width get scaled to be 48px wide, and height gets scaled to 48px tall. Since I'm using a 2px stroke around the edge, that's generally shrinking it down by about 4%.

For clean up, if the icons are intended to have transparent areas, I'll remove the white areas as necessary. And I suppose that's that. They look like line drawings because they are line drawings. :)

My three trade secrets

1. I draw imperfect looking icons because that's all I have the patience and ability to create. The end result is a unique, friendly-looking doodle that I let you colour in. I don't want to say that this is laziness, but more that I bet your colouring in will be way better than my colouring in. Also, you can colour them to work perfectly in each design, rather than having to adjust tints to not make things awkward. Everything is hand-drawn; there are no quick-shape shortcuts. It's the pen and direct selection tools only.

2. All of the circles used in my icons are drawn with three anchor points instead of four. Four gets you a proper perfect circle (if you do it right), but with three there's always something a little off. The best circle I've managed to get with three points is the best that I might hand-draw with pen and paper. Anything better wouldn't fit in the set anyway.

3. My icons are made like you would make cookies. First, you cut out the shape until it looks right, and then you decorate inside with thin frosting lines.

Using colour

So far we've dealt only with pictogram-style icons, the kind we might find in website navigation or a mobile app toolbar. Once we start looking at icons for other contexts like desktop software, we need to start covering the basics of colour, light and perspective.

What colour depth to use?

Colour depth is the number of colours an icon contains, determined by a combination of factors spanning hardware (screen, graphics card) and software (the operating system and colour settings). It's measured in bits: 8-bit, 16-bit, and so on. The higher the bit depth, the more colours that can be displayed.

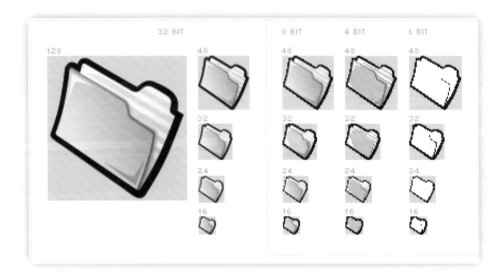

To make things confusing, there are two types of measurement. Each of the primary screen colours (red, green and blue) are channels and the bit depth for each of these is termed bits per channel. This is a colour setting that you will see in photo editors such as Photoshop. The total number of bits available at each pixel (in all three channels) is called bits per pixel, and sometimes 'bpp' is added to make it clear which depth is being referred to. In this book, we'll refer to bits per pixel.

The first computers, like the Mac Classic, were only 1-bit: a pixel was either on or off, black or white, with no grey tones in between. As technology progressed, they were superseded by 4-bit computers, capable of displaying sixteen colours (as there are sixteen different combinations of four bits), and 8-bit, with up to 256 different colours, as used in Mac OS 9 and Windows 95–2000.

While most modern desktop computers and mobile devices support 24-bit colour (16 million colours) or 32-bit (24-bit colour plus an 8-bit alpha channel), some recent mobile devices are still only capable of 16-bit colour (65,536 colours). It still sounds like a lot of colours, but limitations are particularly noticeable in gradients, where unsightly banding will occur instead of a smooth transition. This effect is reduced the smaller the gradient area is.

A way around this banding problem is a technique called dithering, which uses a dot-like effect to give the impression of a gradient.

Noise Dither

Pattern Dither

If you're designing icons intended only for Mac OS X, this won't be a big concern to you, but Windows users may have their display preferences set to sixteen colour (4-bit) mode. When creating icons for a Windows application, such as a toolbar, it still makes sense to include 4-bit images.

As well as differences in colour depth, screens vary in how they display colour, too, which can mean making adjustments to compensate. For instance, when creating icons for Android, desaturating them by 30% will compensate for the oversaturated active matrix AMOLED screens they use.

Light

Once we start looking at colour icons, we're moving into more realistic and less stylised artwork. It now becomes important to think about a consistent lighting direction. To appear natural, the light source should be either directly above, or above and slightly to one side (lack of space for long shadows precludes extreme lighting angles). This decision will change where the highlights and shadows fall on your icons:

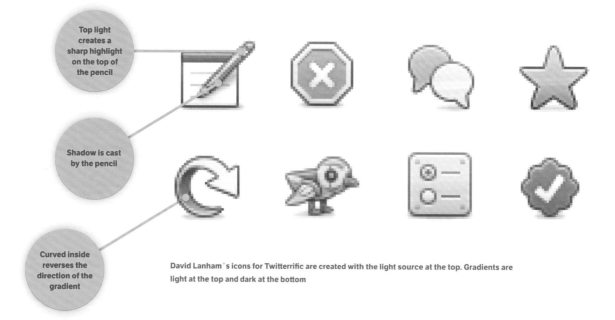

Top light creates a sharp highlight on the top of the pencil

Shadow is cast by the pencil

Curved inside reverses the direction of the gradient

David Lanham´s icons for Twitterrific are created with the light source at the top. Gradients are light at the top and dark at the bottom

This affects not only the the shadows and highlights but also the gradients used on an icon's surface. Subtle gradients will make objects appear less flat and more interesting. The lighter part of the gradient would naturally be at the top, unless something, like the page curl on a document icon, for example, would make it the reverse.

Notice also how these icons have a delicate transparent white inner border. This has the effect of making the borders appear crisper:

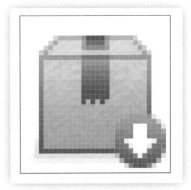

We can also use subtle gradients on the borders too, which almost unnoticeably adds to the overall effect. It's a good rule of thumb that if you are aware of the gradient, it's probably too steep.

The light source doesn't have to be from above though — if you deliberately wanted a spooky effect, the light direction might come from below, or perhaps even within the icon.

If we want the icon to look natural, we must pay heed to colours. I never use 100% black (with the occasional exception of elements such as text that needs to be clear) as it's often too stark in contrast and doesn't look natural. Knocking it back to 90–80% grey has the desired effect. Now look at something that's black and you'll realise that it's not truly 100% black. If the surface is glossy, it will pick up and reflect colours around it, such as the blue sky or green grass. If the surface is silver, you might get both of those colours!

Observation is the key and having a reference, either real or photographic, will help enormously. One huge advantage that I have drawing now, compared to when I was painting wildlife with acrylics, is that I can sample colours from digital images easily. You'll need to use your judgement as to whether the sampled colour looks right, as colours are affected by light conditions and surrounding objects, but it's a great timesaver.

Draw, pardner! №2: This time in colour!

Let's draw another icon: this time we're going to be dealing with colour, light and a little perspective. I've taken as an example a 32px downloads icon for a toolbar, with an accompanying 16px version to be used in a sidebar. This time we won't be detailing the minutiae of x- and y-co-ordinates and vector sizes; instead we'll concentrate on the elements that make up the icon.

The common metaphor used for downloads is the parcel or cardboard box with a down arrow for extra clarity. Hopefully, we're all designers who can appreciate the beauty of cardboard! The 32px icon will afford us room for some subtle detail, but we'll make the 16px version much simpler.

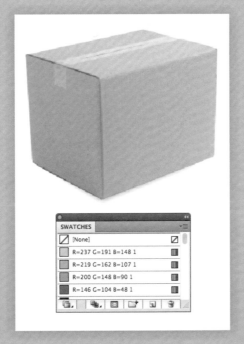

Step 1: To start, I found a good photograph of a cardboard box online, in which three sides were visible, each with its own tone. I sampled these colours, as well as the dark gap at the top of the box, and saved them as swatches for use later. The photo will also act as a reference.

Step 2: Starting with the front face of the box, let's draw a rectangle and add the three sampled colours to it as a gradient fill. We won't show every part of the gradient in one shape as the contrast would be too extreme.

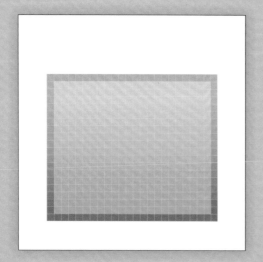

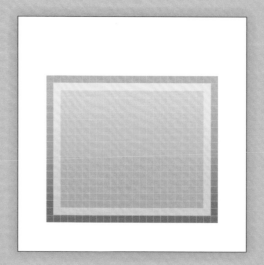

Step 3: Now, we'll add the outer border. Apps like Photoshop let you specify a gradient stroke, but in Illustrator we'll have to draw a new shape behind to achieve the same effect. You could also use a little workaround: in the appearance palette, add a new fill underneath the current one (Effect → Path → Offset Path). Specify the offset by the width of the border (in this case, 1px). This is handy if for some reason you really need to have the border on the same path but, for this exercise, a separate vector shape is the simplest.

For the top of the border gradient, we'll use the colour sample from the darkest side of the box, and for the bottom, the one taken from the gap.

Step 4: Next, we'll add the inner white border, including a 1px white stroke with an opacity of 35% to crispen it up.

Step 5: These shapes are then repeated for the back of the box. Here, we're just going to use simple one-point perspective so that it doesn't look out of place with other icons that are completely face-on. The little suggestion of depth will just help it be recognisable.

First we'll duplicate the border shape, reduce it to 4px high, and bring in the top corner anchor points by 4px to give it a foreshortening effect.

Step 6: Then we'll do the same for the main shapes on top, except there's tweaking to be done to make the border visible. The height is reduced to 3px (we only want the border to show at the top, not the bottom as well), and the sides are brought in by 2px.

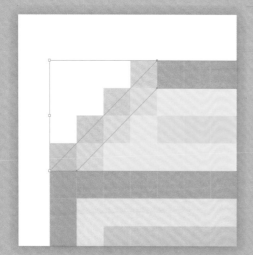

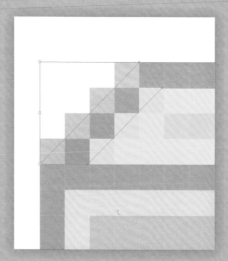

As you can see in this comparison, the nature of anti-aliasing at 1px means that the border is barely visible.

We'll also adjust the gradient to show the lighter portion, as this part of the box will be getting the most light.

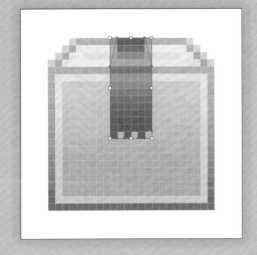

Step 7: The basic box is now drawn and it's time to add the details. First, we want to add a subtle noise texture to break up the flatness of the colour. We could apply this directly to the shapes, but that wouldn't give us much control over the strength of the effect. Instead, we'll copy the shapes, fill them with white, apply the simplest possible film grain noise (grain at 1; highlight and intensity set to 0), and give it a transparency of multiply. This leaves just the darker noise pixels and we can tweak the opacity until we're happy with how strong it is. In this case, 80% did the trick.

Step 8: When it comes to drawing the tape, we won't follow the clear tape shown in the reference. It needs to be more obvious, so we'll go for the dark brown tape instead. As a little detail, we'll add a crenellation pattern to the bottom, which from a distance will give it an impression of a serrated edge from a tape cutter. It doesn't matter that this is actually out of scale as exaggerating this element adds to the overall impression.

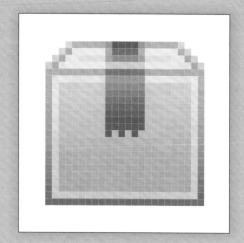

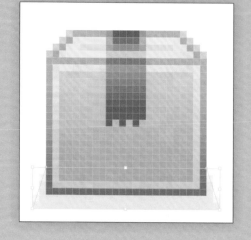

As the tape is glossy, we shouldn't add any noise or texture; instead, we'll add a small white rectangle with 40% opacity to the edge going around the box, just to give a suggestion of glossiness.

Step 9: The shadow is drawn by creating a similar shape to the top of the box. This is filled with black and given an opacity of only 15%.

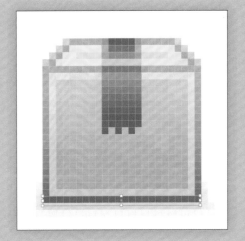

It looks too sharp to be a shadow at the moment, but applying a Gaussian blur filter would be too much for this shadow. We can get a more suitable effect by simply making the shape's anchor point sit between pixels.

To finish it off, we'll add a further shadow to the very bottom of the box, a black rectangle with 15% opacity that overlaps the bottom, darkening the bottom of the border, as well as the area of shadow right underneath the box.

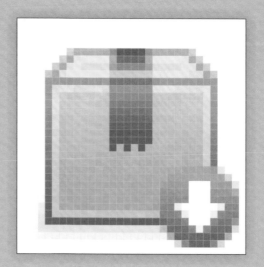

As the final touch, we can add a modifier to show various states, such as download in progress. The inner margin we left also helps the modifier to overlap the base icon, making it stand out.

Once the icon is complete, there are usually some final tweaks to take care of. For example, I felt that the border on the front of the box wasn't quite strong enough.

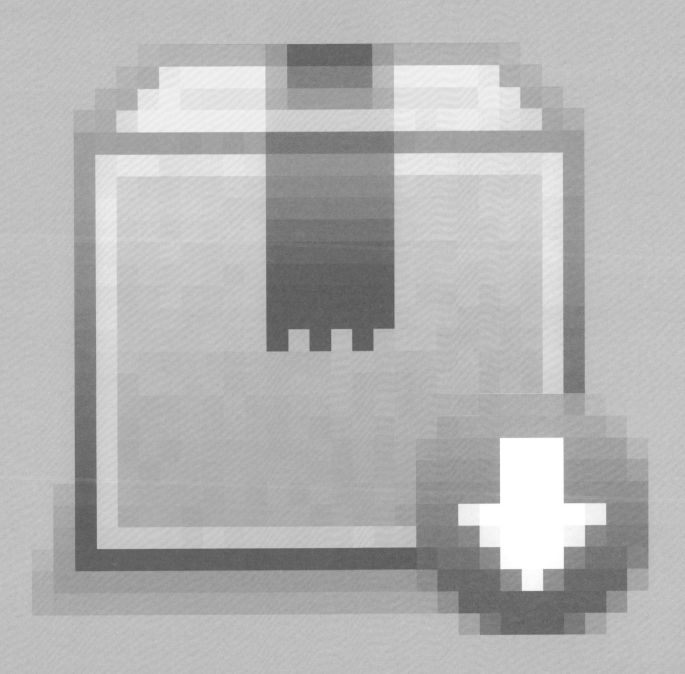

DoubleTwist icons by Sebastiaan de With

Sebastiaan de With originally started off as a freelance designer, working for both small independent software developers and large corporations. In 2011 he became chief creative officer for doubleTwist, a cross-platform application for managing and syncing music, photos and videos. In addition to discussing his workflow, I was particularly keen to know more about the work Sebastiaan had done for the Android platform and how different it was to design for.

With desktop and mobile versions of doubleTwist, how transferable were the icons? Did you have to redraw anything to work in a particular context?

Very much so. Apart from the obvious changes between the dynamics of a mobile screen and a desktop screen — the typically higher pixel density, the cramped screen real estate and the typical distance of the eye to the display — the Android phones that have most of the market today achieve a high amount of pixels per inch by reducing the amount of coloured subpixels. A subpixel is essentially a small coloured light: three of them (red, green and blue) typically make up one pixel. With Android phones, every other pixel misses either a blue or green subpixel to squeeze more pixels into the same area. The result is a kind of grainy screen, which also makes the edges of the white-on-black icons noticeably jaggy. I had to figure out a way to activate particular subpixels along the edges of the icons to make them appear smooth!

What differences did you find designing for Android compared to Mac or iOS?

There was the elephant in the room of making things look too much like iOS or the aesthetic that's generally associated with Apple. While doubleTwist has always been unique in its visual styling, having as much as a sidebar in the Mac app or a layer of gloss on an interface element was enough to ignite a discussion on internet forums where people would accuse us of copying Apple.

What is your workflow? What tools do you use (and what do you like about them), and how do you arrive at the final icon?

Like a lot of my colleagues, I only use Photoshop and occasionally Cinema4D for complex icons that need 3-D rendering. Photoshop has all the vector tools I need to build scalable, adjustable icons, but it's still geared towards making actual pixel output. For all of Photoshop's flaws, it is actually quite usable for this purpose, though there are a lot of things that can be improved upon. It's a real shame there is no true tool made for creating icons and UI elements with vector shapes.

When designing icons, I usually start out with rough sketches on paper and, once I get some solid ideas and metaphors down, I move to Photoshop and start pushing bezier curves and pixels around. Then, iterate until golden and crispy!

The standard media player controls are established icon conventions, but were there any icons that were more complex to create? How do you decide what metaphor to use?

 Certainly. For one, I had to fit icons for features like AirPlay and UPnP streaming, and the visual EQ into that control area, which includes the very standardised audio playback icons.

For most of these, I went with the 'mom test'. I did several designs and tried to see if my colleagues recognised it as the intended feature. Then I proceeded to test it with my mother. And my wife's mother. When they were able to recognise it as an icon for playback over the air (or wireless playback), I knew I'd succeeded.

Were there any technical challenges to overcome, such as with the variations in the hardware?

When you design a mobile app, there's already a lot of factors to take into account, like in what situations and settings users interact with your app, but designing for Android means adding quite a few more factors to take into consideration. I've designed various sizes of each resource, at various scaling factors (none of the niceness of Apple's iOS 1× or 2× scaling here!), and tested colours, edge aliasing and other factors on a variety of screen technologies to make sure things look good. That's not even counting ensuring the layout of a UI is variable because screen aspect ratios and sizes vary. It's... a challenge!

ARTISTS

ALBUMS

Summary

In this chapter we've looked at the general techniques involved in drawing icons, but each context has its own specific requirements and artwork styles. For instance, when creating toolbar, navigation or tab bar icons for iOS, you don't need to worry about selecting the correct colour and making an image for each state. iOS uses the alpha channel from your image and automatically displays the correct colour and any highlight or shadow effect.

For more information on creating icons for specific contexts and their requirements, consult the comprehensive icon reference chart in the appendix.

Now that we've created some icons, the next step is choosing the correct file format and then, in the case of the web, deployment.

Chapter reference

doubleTwist
http://www.doubletwist.com/

Bitmap fonts
http://www.dafont.com/4mini.font
http://www.dafont.com/nokia-cellphone.font

Further reading

Bit depth tutorial
http://www.cambridgeincolour.com/tutorials/bit-depth.htm

Veerle's blog
http://veerle.duoh.com
A fantastic source of Adobe Illustrator drawing tutorials, showing you how to construct complex shapes and patterns, as well as blogging on design in general.

Chapter 6

Icon formats and deployment —

the technical guide

There are a number of different formats of, and methods for, deploying icons, and while PNG is undeniably the most common, there are others with their own particular pros and cons that are useful if the context is right. We've briefly touched on this in Chapter 3 with regards to favicons, but now we'll look at all the other contexts. The format we choose can also have some bearing on the creation of the artwork, so it's worth considering this before getting started.

As well as covering the pros and cons of each format, and how it affects the artwork, we'll also look at the variety of techniques for displaying icons on the web.

Modern challenges of icon creation

One context in particular that we're going to have to bear in mind for the future is the challenge of resolution independence.

As technology is ever improving, screen densities are increasing, and we're going to be faced with a sizing problem. We've already felt the first effects of this with designing for screens like the iPhone 4, which has double the pixel density of the previous generation and requires icons to be produced at the same initial resolution (72 dpi) but at twice the size:

57px (right) is large enough for older iOS devices, but looks rubbish on a retina display compared to the 114px version (left)

The difference is astounding — finally screen graphics are obtaining the crispness of print. Back in the days of 15" monitors with resolutions of 800×600px, the individual pixels were obvious, but now I use a Macbook Air that has a 13" screen with 1,440×900 pixels. Those squares are becoming invisible.

There's another aspect to resolution independence, which is zooming. Now that all major browsers can zoom content, rather than just increase the text size, bitmap images immediately start to look like rubbish when enlarged. We need to create artwork that can be scaled without losing quality.

Ugh! Look at that state of these icons and Logo when the browser is zoomed in!

There are currently two solutions to this problem: packaging multiple different-sized bitmaps in one container format such as .ico or .icns; or a single vector file such as PDF or SVG. It would seem that a vector format would be ideal for icons: after all, a single file could be resized without losing quality. However, the more complex a vector image is, the larger it's file size and the longer it takes for a graphics processing unit to process it. Bitmap images need much less processing, though, and for complex illustrations the file size can be dramatically smaller too.

It's also not always possible to create one vector image that can be scaled up or down for anything particularly complex. The larger an icon is, the more detail it potentially needs, and the smaller it is, the less it needs. A large colour icon such as an application icon will contain detail that becomes a fuzzy mess when reduced. For pixel optimisation, it still has to be a bitmap.

Compare the specially designed 16px icon for xScope (centre) with the 512px version simply resized to 16px (right). We still need to specify optimised bitmaps for the smaller sizes to get the best quality

For simple monochrome pictograms, however, vectors do work and these will be covered later.

Finally, we can't talk about resolution independence without a particular app that has been designed for this specific purpose: Opacity. A Mac-only graphics editor, it simplifies the process of creating multiple resolutions of an icon, and also makes it possible to add another size easily at a later date.

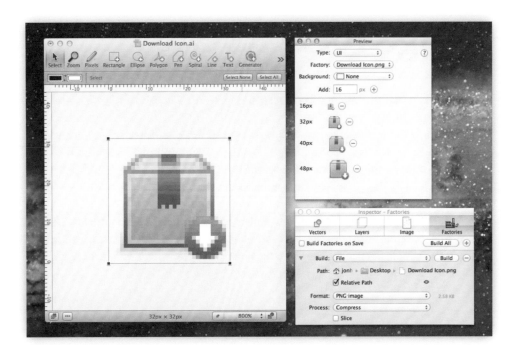

On a simple level, we could start with an icon at 32px, and then add 64px, with Opacity creating the artwork for us. If we need more control, layers (such as those containing details) can be hidden at certain resolutions, and we can alter values such as stroke widths if we don't just want a straight enlargement. Finally, Opacity can export the artwork in multiple formats at the same time: PNG, SVG and PDF being the key ones here. It also has the ability to export to JavaScript for use with the `<canvas>` element.

With these challenges in mind, let's look at the possible formats and deployment methods.

Image formats

PNG (Portable Network Graphics)

If we're making an icon for screen use, be it for a website or an app interface, the chances are that it will be a PNG. It supports more colours than GIF, as well as the all-important alpha transparency, which allows for smooth edges.

How it affects our artwork

Not much! We'll be hard-pressed to find a graphics editor that doesn't export to PNG, but we may find it useful to run our PNGs through an optimiser, such as PNG Crush, to ensure the smallest possible file size. It does this by removing unnecessary metadata, or reducing the colour depth if a 256-colour palette can be used.

GIF (Graphics Interchange Format)

It's unlikely that we would choose this older format over the more modern and ubiquitous PNG, but there are some cases where it's still useful, namely animation. While PNG can be animated (in the form of APNG), support for it is limited, whereas everything supports animated GIFs, without the need for a plugin. Also, if image transparency in IE6 is required, we will have to make a GIF version of the artwork, although the chances of needing this are becoming smaller every year.

How it affects our artwork

As GIF doesn't support alpha transparency, we'll need to make edges aliased. We'll also need to restrict artwork to 256 colours, or at least check that it doesn't look bonkers when exported as a GIF.

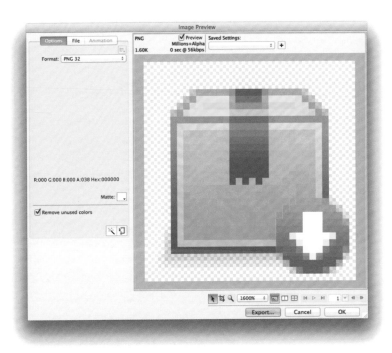

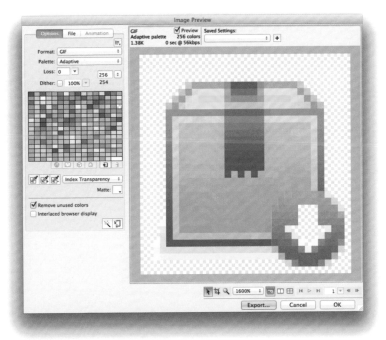

TIFF (Tagged Image File Format)

While TIFF isn't a format we'd use on the web, it is a useful format when creating icons for the Mac OS X interface, due to it's ability to contain several icon sizes in one file (known as a multipage TIFF). We can use the command line TIFF utility (tiffutil) in Terminal.app to combine multiple TIFF images into one, like this:

```
tiffutil -cat icon32px.tiff icon24px.tiff -out icon.tiff
```

The first two images are the separate 32px and 24px icons, and then the name (and location) of the combined file is specified after the `-out`. This has been used to support default and small sizes for Mac OS X toolbar icons. You can also use IconBuilder or MultiTiff, an online app, to create multipage TIFFs.

How it affects our artwork
The only thing to watch for is whether our choice of editor supports exporting to TIFF format — the major ones certainly do.

SVG (Scalable Vector Graphics)

Whereas PNG, GIF and TIFF are all bitmap formats, SVG is an XML file describing the vector information and making it scalable. There have been two main factors holding back the adoption of this useful format. The first is the historic lack of support in Internet Explorer. The other came when Adobe dropped support for SVG in 2008, preferring to promote Flash. However, while desktop support has lagged behind, it's been steadily growing as an ideal format for mobile devices and now, with the introduction of SVG support in IE9, it will reach an even wider audience. Opera currently has the best implementation and even uses it for some elements in it's UI. If you ever need to view an SVG file, use Opera.

It is also worth knowing that, as Mac OS X has a graphics layer capable of displaying PDF, Linux distributions make good use of SVG. Variants of Linux that ship with the Elementary icon set (Ubuntu, Xubuntu, Lubuntu, Elementary, Pinguy, and so on) use SVG for all their icons (while GNOME still uses PNG), but we'll look more into that in chapter 7.

Let's look at an example of SVG:

This simple play icon is created by the following XML:

```
<?xml version="1.0" encoding="utf-8"?>
<!DOCTYPE svg PUBLIC "-//W3C//DTD SVG 1.1//EN" "http://www.w3.org/Graphics/
SVG/1.1/DTD/svg11.dtd">

<svg version="1.1" xmlns="http://www.w3.org/2000/svg" xmlns:xlink="http://www.
w3.org/1999/xlink" x="0px" y="0px" width="16px" height="16px">
<polygon points="2,0 2,16 15.5,8" id="play" />
</svg>
```

Note that the object can be assigned an ID, meaning that it can be accessed and manipulated with JavaScript and CSS as part of the DOM tree (to carry out actions such as changing icon colours, for example).

Also, unlike PDF, it can use filters like gaussian blur without using bitmaps:

```
<?xml version="1.0" encoding="utf-8"?>
<!DOCTYPE svg PUBLIC "-//W3C//DTD SVG 1.1//EN" "http://www.w3.org/Graphics/
SVG/1.1/DTD/svg11.dtd">
<svg version="1.1" xmlns="http://www.w3.org/2000/svg" xmlns:xlink="http://www.
w3.org/1999/xlink" x="0px" y="0px" width="16px" height="24px" viewBox="0 0 16 24"
enable-background="new 0 0 16 24" xml:space="preserve">

<filter  id="ShadowBlur">
    <feGaussianBlur  stdDeviation="0.4"></feGaussianBlur>
</filter>

<g filter="url(#ShadowBlur)">
    <ellipse opacity="0.2" enable-background="new      " cx="7.375" cy="16.062"
rx="6.375" ry="0.938"/>
</g>

<g>
    <polygon id="play" points="1,0 1,16 14.5,8"/>
</g>
</svg>
```

SVG icons can be created in a number of applications, most notably the open source
graphics editor Inkscape, which actually uses SVG as it's native format. Other apps have
the option to export to SVG, such as Adobe Illustrator, but the XML markup often needs
editing to reduce bloat. It's worth optimising SVG file output, as it helps file size
and performance.

How it affects our artwork

While some graphics apps can specify strokes inside or outside a path, SVG only supports a centred stroke. One workaround is to convert the stroke to a filled path before export. In Illustrator, any area where a filter has been used (such as gaussian blur) that isn't explicitly an SVG filter will be output as bitmaps. SVG can reference external bitmaps and display them, but if the intention is purely vector artwork, this isn't desired.

There are different specifications of SVG, and not every device supports the latest stable spec (currently this is version 1.1). For example, some phones can use SVG-Tiny, a smaller, simpler subset of SVG, thereby saving memory. If we've been asked to provide SVG icons, we will need to check what version we need to work to.

Cleanliness of exported SVG code varies with each app. Some will add a lot of extraneous metadata, but converting text to paths and using a single layer can help avoid some of it.

SVG doesn't handle artwork smaller than a pixel very well, as it becomes much less visible than it would on the equivalent bitmap image.

Canvas

Whereas the heart of SVG is an XML text file, canvas is a JavaScript API allowing you to programatically draw on to a bitmap image, and is therefore only intended for use on the web. It was implemented initially by Apple inside WebKit, for use in Safari and Dashboard widgets, but the format has been adopted by other browsers, including IE9.

Being a bitmap, canvas is not a scalable format. It's advantage lies in the fact that colour can be chosen via JavaScript. This colour flexibility does help with icon reuse, but the reality is that canvas is too fiddly to work with for icon design. Unlike SVG, there are precious few graphic editors that can export artwork in this format, and those that do (such as Opacity) output code that is much larger than an equivalent SVG or PNG file. It's a lot of hassle and, with no scalability, we're better off with one of the other formats discussed in this chapter.

There is an alternative, however, called Raphaël, a JavaScript library that renders vector graphics based on the SVG spec. All the advantages of SVG (scalable and exists in the DOM) but with better cross-browser compatibility!

It's only real downside is that it can't (yet) take SVG code directly (as we would want to create artwork in something like Illustrator, rather than by writing code) but, at the time of writing, there are tools in the works that will convert the SVG for us: *http://readysetraphael.com/*. It's an extra step, and it doesn't support everything available in SVG, but the promise of good browser support might make it worth it.

How it affects our artwork

The most likely workflow with Raphaël is to convert SVG files, exported from a graphics editor, rather than create icons directly with code. Therefore, the rules are the same as with SVG.

PDF

While not a suitable format for icon design on the web (at the moment), PDF is becoming very useful in software as it's supported by Quartz, the graphics layer in Mac OS X. Traditionally a format thought of as just a means of sending text documents around, PDF actually retains vector information and can be used interchangeably in Adobe Illustrator with it's own native format (.ai). Apps like Coda (below) and Google Chrome have already shown that for simple, scalable icons, it can be a handy format.

While complex application icons served as PDF would result in too large a file, for icons like this it's ideal. File sizes vary: the Coda icon weighs in at 22Kb, whereas the Google Chrome icon is down to the low of 6Kb. So while it is a bit heavier than the bitmap version, it's infinitely scalable.

How it affects our artwork

The requirement to export as PDF, retaining vector information, will restrict our tool choices to Illustrator, Opacity or OmniGraffle. It works best to create the artwork at the actual size that it will used at, and then scale it up from there.

Displaying icons on websites

When deploying icons in software such as a desktop or Android app, deployment isn't really a concern. We create the .png, .ico or .icns and the code does the rest. For websites, however, there are a few different techniques, each with their own pros and cons.

The traditional way to include images is in the HTML of the page, using the `<img>` element. While this is good for actual page content (such as photos and diagrams), it's not as suitable for icons, which usually support the content, rather than being content themselves. For instance, when using icons to support navigation, the text content is already there and having an image as well isn't necessary. It is therefore more appropriate to include them as CSS background images.

There are two main challenges regarding the use of icons on websites. First, loading lots of separate images means multiple HTTP requests that will slow down the performance of our sites. It makes sense, then, to cut down the number of requests and reuse icons where possible.

The second challenge is one of scale. All modern browsers allow us to zoom a page, and while the text will scale well, a bitmap icon won't. There's also the tricky subject of resolution independence, as those designing for the iPhone 4 have already discovered.

Here are some different techniques for working smarter and tackling these challenges.

CSS sprites

While CSS sprites aren't technically a format, many high-traffic sites, such as Twitter, use them to reduce bandwidth and HTTP requests, and in so doing increase speed. To create a sprite, we can combine several icons into one single image file by laying them out in a grid. Then, we use different values of the CSS `background-position` property to show each icon.

CSS sprites are also useful for showing different states of the same icon (`:hover`, `:focus` or `:active`) particularly in Internet Explorer 6 or earlier that don't pre-fetch images specified on `:hover`.

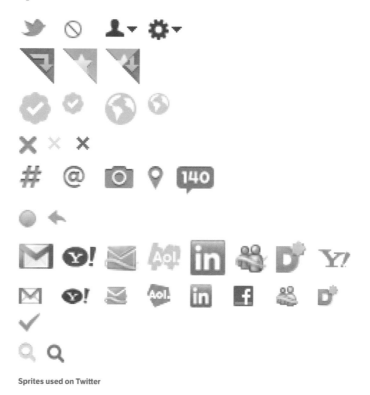

Sprites used on Twitter

Here's some typical CSS sprite code — first our HTML:

```
<a href="/settings/" class="icon settings">
  Settings
</a>
```

You'll have noticed that we added two — yes, two — class attribute values to that anchor: icon and settings. More about those in just a minute.

Now for the CSS:

```
.icon {
  display: block;
  width: 16px;
  height: 16px;
  overflow: hidden;
  background-image: url(sprite.png);
  background-repeat: no-repeat;
}

.settings {
  background-position: 32px -48px;
}
```

So, why did we add those two class attribute values? With the first, icon, we'll define styles shared among many elements. With the second, settings, we'll apply different background-position values for each icon. But what do those icon styles do?

Put simply, block level elements such as divisions, headings and paragraphs create a new line in the normal flow of any webpage and can be given dimensions like width and height. Inline — or text-level — elements like spans, anchors and text formatting (such as <em> and <strong>) don't. Unless, that is, we change that display behaviour using CSS.

First, we'll apply `display:block;` to our text-level anchor to enable us to specify a `width` and a `height`. Then, we'll add `overflow:hidden;` to make sure only the icon we want to see is visible. Next, we specify the path to our sprite image and set it to `no-repeat`. Finally, we set the CSS `background-position` for individual icons. In this instance, we are setting 32px from the left (X) and -48px from the top (Y), using a negative value to move it up.

Another advantage of using CSS sprites is that they make the alignment of icons with text easier than it is with inline images. With sprites, you can change image states consistently and it fits well with the practice of designing icons together.

Using CSS sprites has many advantages but there are disadvantages, too. Here are some, along with possible solutions:

- **The more icons you need, the more complex writing CSS** `background-position` **rules becomes.**

Lay out icons in a single column, so that you need change only the Y-axis values in your style sheet.

- **If the size of text changes, or the page is zoomed, neighbouring icons in the grid can sometimes appear.**

Allow plenty of space between icons and choose a grid size that makes calculating their positions easier. For example, if 16px icons with 4px breathing space between them are placed 20px apart, the Y-position of the fourth icon would simply be -80px.

Adding extra breathing space between icons helps reduce the likelihood of unwanted icons appearing, but it will also increase the physical size of the complete sprite image.

- **We can't add** `alt` **text to CSS background images. If we're relying on icons to convey information, that information will be lost.**

To help CSS sprites remain accessible, we can include meaningful text content in HTML and then move it out of sight using CSS.

```
<a href="/settings/" class="icon settings">
  Settings
</a>
```

Now we'll hide that text by moving it off the left side of the screen with `text-indent`:

```
.icon {
  text-indent: -999em;
  overflow: hidden;
  display:block;
  width: 18px;
  height: 18px;
}
```

- **When we change just one icon, we must change the entire sprite image.**

Creating and applying CSS sprites can sometimes be tricky and the solution is far from perfect but, on balance, I think that that the pros far outweigh the cons.

High resolution replacements

The density of pixels in the Retina display on the iPhone 4, 4S and latest generation iPod Touch means that standard resolution icons will look decidedly rough alongside crisp text in our websites or apps.

To avoid this, we can produce artwork at the same initial resolution (72dpi) but at twice the size. Then we use the CSS background-size property to visually shrink those icons so they look the same size on all screens but contain twice the pixel information on Retina displays.

View these examples online at http://iconhandbook.co.uk/reference/examples/retina/

CSS3 media queries make it possible to detect higher resolution displays and then serve an image that's double in size to those screens. Here's the current method for doing this to provide support for platforms other than iOS:

```
@media="only screen and (-webkit-min-device-pixel-ratio: 1.5), only screen and
(-o-min-device-pixel-ratio: 3/2), only screen and (min-device-pixel-ratio: 1.5) {

.icon {
  background-image: url(iconx2.png);
  background-size: 150px 40px;
}
```

What about inline content images written into our markup? Can we replace these with a higher resolution version too? Yes, with a little CSS.

```
img.icon {
  background-image: url(iconx2.png);
  background-repeat: no-repeat;
  background-size: 150px 40px;
  height: 0;
  width: 0;
  padding: 22px 0 0 22px;
  overflow:hidden;
}
```

Let's break this technique down. First, we'll set both the `height` and the `width` of the image to zero. Why? Because next, we'll create those dimensions again by using top and left `padding`. This padding will also push the image right and down and out of sight. Because we set `overflow:hidden`, only the CSS background image will remain visible.

Data URIs

It's possible to encode a bitmap image into Base64, also known as a data URI. Instead of referencing an external image file, Base64 code is embedded into a style sheet and interpreted by a browser which then displays the encoded image. For example, here is an icon converted into a data URI for use in HTML and CSS.

Original icon

Data URI in HTML

```
<img width="32" height="32" title="" alt="" src="data:image/png;base64,iVBORw0KGgo
AAAANSUhEUgAAACAAAAAgCAYAA
ABzenr0AAAAGXRFWHRTb2Z0d2FyZQBBZG9iZSBJbWFnZVJlYWR5ccllPAAAAI1
JREFUeNpiZhhgwDzQDmDCIiYAxPuB+D+NMEFAS8uJcgBMYQOVQxurA5gGOg0
w4nApNc1gRBNjHFQhMOqAUQeMOmDUAdRygAEQ34fSVKs0iMUgS99D2e+hfG
y1H8m1IbH4PQE+XgdQozIitrIarYxGHTDqgFEHEO2AAzRsgTMSo5DaXbPBDQa8
dwwQYABhUXbH2+HtUgAAAABJRU5ErkJggg==" />
```

Data URI in CSS

```
.bookmark {
background(data:image/png;base64,iVBORw0KGgoAAAANSUhEUgAAAC
AAAAAgCAYAAABzenr0AAAAGXRFWHRTb2Z0d2FyZQBBZG9iZSBJbWFnZVJlYW
R5ccllPAAAAI1JREFUeNpiZhhgwDzQDmDCIiYAxPuB+D+NMEFAS8uJcgBMYQOV
QxurA5gGOg0w4nApNc1gRBNjHFQhMOqAUQeMOmDUAdRygAEQ34fSVKs0iMU
gS99D2e+hfGy1H8m1IbH4PQE+XgdQozIitrIarYxGHTDqgFEHEO2AAzRsgTMSo5
DaXbPBDQa8dwwQYABhUXbH2+HtUgAAAABJRU5ErkJggg==)
}
```

Data URIs can come in very handy:

- They reduce HTTP requests, meaning faster load times, as only one file needs to be downloaded.

- When creating site-specific user styles or themes, such as my Helvetireader theme for Google Reader, icons can be embedded into the style sheet, making a theme more easily transportable.

- Images can be embedded in HTML emails without them needing to be attached or referenced from a remote source.

- Firefox doesn't allow local images to be used in site-specific style sheets, so embedding data URI images into a style sheet works around that problem.

  We don't need any special tools to create data URI images and there are excellent services available online from sites such as Web Semantics.

Data URI images sound great, don't they? But are there drawbacks? Unfortunately, yes.

- Filenames are no longer human-readable, so you'll need to comment your CSS to identify each icon.

- Complex images mean more code, more visual noise and style sheets that are more difficult to scan when editing.

- There are no file size benefits. In fact, data URI encoded images can be 30% larger on average.

- Each time you update an icon, you'll need to reconvert it to Base64. You can avoid this by converting them on the fly, server-side. However, doing this will increase CPU load on your server.

- Internet Explorer versions 7 and below don't support data URI encoded images. If support for this legacy browser is essential, then data URIs aren't the right solution.

Context is everything, of course, but if you have only a few icons or a site or app with themes, data URIs could be well worth considering.

Icons as fonts

Fonts are a largely untapped format for deploying icons on websites, but they solve the problem of scaling with hinting, where a font is designed to line up with a pixel grid to enable readability (or crispness in the case of icons) at small sizes.

One common complaint about using fonts for icons is that it can mean adding a meaningless character to our markup. We can overcome this by using CSS generated content — on it's own or in combination with the `data-icon` attribute — to keep our markup minimal and meaningful.

Our simple markup looks like this:

```
<a href="/basket" class="icon basket">View Basket</a>
```

Did you notice those multiple class attributes again? Next, we'll import our font using the `@font-face` web fonts property in CSS:

```
@font-face {
  font-family: 'Pictos';
  src: url('pictos-web.eot');
  src: local('☺'),
  url('pictos-web.woff') format('woff'),
  url('pictos-web.ttf') format('truetype'),
  url('pictos-web.svg#webfontIyfZbseF') format('svg');
}
```

This rather complicated looking set of rules is (at the time of writing) the most bulletproof way of ensuring as many browsers as possible load the font we want. We'll now use the `content` property applied to the `:before` pseudo-element selector to generate our icon. Once again, we'll use those multiple class attribute values to set common `icon` styles, then specific styles for `basket`. This helps us avoid repeating styles:

```
.icon {
  font-family: 'Pictos';
  font-size: 22px:
}

.basket:before {
  content: "$";
}
```

What does the `:before` pseudo-class do? It generates the dollar character in a browser, even when it's not present in the markup. Using the generated content approach means our markup stays simple, but we'll need a new line of CSS, defining what letter to apply to each `class` attribute, for every icon we add.

197

`data-icon` is a new alternative approach that uses the HTML5 `data-` attribute in combination with CSS attribute selectors. This new attribute lets us add our own metadata to elements, as long as it's prefixed by `data-` and doesn't contain any uppercase letters. In this case we want to use it to provide the letter value for the icon. Look closely at this markup and you'll see the `data-icon` attribute.

```
<a href="/basket" class="icon" data-icon="$">View Basket</a>
```

🛒 View Basket (2 items)

We could add others, in fact as many as we like.

```
<a href="/" class="icon" data-icon="k">Favourites</a>
<a href="/" class="icon" data-icon="t">History</a>
<a href="/" class="icon" data-icon="@">Location</a>
```

View these examples online at
http://iconhandbook.co.uk/reference/examples/pictos/

♥ Favourites   🕓 History   📍 Location

Then we need just one CSS attribute selector to style all our icons in one go:

```
.icon:before {
  content: attr(data-icon);
}
```

By placing our custom attribute `data-icon` in the selector in this way, we can enable CSS to read the value of that attribute and display it before the element (in this case, the anchor tag). It's worth pointing out that in both of these approaches, the letter will be announced to people using screen readers.

A great example of this type of delivery is Drew Wilson's Pictos icon set. He spent a great deal of time researching and testing Pictos, giving him a wealth of experience and knowledge of the advantages and disadvantages of using fonts to deploy icons.

Pictos font

What made you create an icon font in the first place?

One of the awesome people who bought my Pictos icons had emailed me a sample of three Pictos icons turned into a font. I told them it was a fantastic idea and so I immediately got to work building a custom font for Pictos. Seeing the huge potential in using a font and CSS to render icons made it a no-brainer to spend the time to create it.

What was your workflow? Did you have to change your drawing style in any way?

All my glyphs were already in Illustrator, since Pictos is also vector icons, so I brought them one by one into FontLab Studio (an expensive piece of software but worth it). Then I used Font Squirrel to generate the web font versions.

Did you explore the use of font hinting to make the font work at specific sizes?

Font Squirrel does some of that for you. The hinting language is something totally new to me and I really have no time to get good enough at it to make any real improvements. It is also extraordinarily time-consuming, and would make the price of Pictos go up. In the end, I don't think it would be worth it for Pictos. The font renders just like the Illustrator vectors in WebKit. Now we just need to wait for the other browsers to catch up and we get automatic beautification :)

Would you update the Pictos font in the future with new glyphs?

Yes :) In fact I'm already working on a new system that will enable anyone to build their own Pictos font by picking and choosing only the icons they want. This will enable you to keep the font file size as small as possible by including only the icons you need for your design. It will be great for people working on multiple projects that require a different combination of icons for each project. They will be able to generate a custom font for each project :)

What do you see as the benefits of using a font to deliver icons?

The benefits are huge, and right now outweigh the drawbacks in many cases.

- *Load speed and file size*
  Typically, you use image sprites to render icons on the web. If you have a hover state and an active (pressed) state for those icons, your sprite will be three times larger than it needs to be. By using a font instead, you can load in the icons once and use CSS to change their look for hover and active states. Not only that, but a font made up of twelve icons will have a smaller file size than an image sprite with the same number of icons.

- *Scalability*
  Image sprites cannot be scaled up. Vectors or fonts can. By using a font to render your icons, you can scale them to any size and they will not lose any quality.

- *Design on the fly*
  Using a font to render icons enables you to change the look and feel of your icons on the fly using CSS. This is extremely useful and powerful when changing or updating your interface via user interaction or for creating themes.

- *Browser support*
  Custom fonts are supported on all modern browsers; IE supports them all the way back to version 4!

How does the size of the Pictos font compare to bitmaps?

Depends on how big your image sprite is and which browser you are on. The font will be served up in a variety of formats depending on the browser the user is using. For example, the .ttf font is 18Kb. The .woff font is 12Kb, SVG is 41Kb, Base64 CSS file is 42 Kb. All those font file sizes are from my stock Pictos font that contains 94 individual icons. That's a lot! :) When I release the pick and choose font builder, file sizes will be drastically smaller since you will probably not need 94 icons for one project :) In any case, the file sizes you get from a font will usually always be smaller than a transparent image sprite.

The pros of using icon fonts are very compelling, but there are disadvantages too:

- All browsers will display font icons, but each does it slightly differently, resulting in the need to write remedial styles if you want cross-browser, pixel-perfection.

- Icons can only be rendered in monochrome or with a gradient fill in browsers that are capable of rendering CSS3 gradients. Specific parts of the icon can't be a different colour.

- Font icons are only appropriate when there is an accompanying text to provide meaning.

- Without hinting, icons won't align to the pixel grid, especially at small sizes. Luckily, when screen resolutions increase, this won't be an issue.

- Creating an icon font can be a complex and time-consuming process. While font editors can carry out hinting automatically, the best results are achieved manually.

- Browsers support different font formats, so we need several formats.

- Whereas browsers have wide support for web fonts, Internet Explorer has only partial support for pseudo selectors in version 8, and full support from version 9. JavaScript libraries such as Selectivizr can help by bootstrapping support for these selectors.

Despite these minor disadvantages, the advantages of icon fonts outweigh them. As an icon format they have huge potential.

CSS3 masks

CSS3 masks are — at least at the time of writing — supported only by WebKit browsers, but that shouldn't stop us learning about and using them. In the mask syntax we specify either a PNG or SVG format image, or even a CSS3-generated gradient to use as a mask. Where that mask is black, whatever is behind that mask will be revealed, so we can change the colour of an icon simply by changing it's background colour in CSS. Here's that CSS3 mask.

View these examples online at http://iconhandbook.co.uk/reference/examples/imagemask/

```
.icon {
  -webkit-mask-box-image: url(icon.png);
}
```

Current support for CSS3 masks means it might be suitable only for iOS or Android web apps, but as a fallback for non-WebKit browsers, you could use a transparent PNG in combination with CSS background colour.

As long as the non-icon areas are given a colour that matches their surroundings, you'll get the same effect, although this becomes more fiddly when used on top of textures, gradients or patterns. We must also allow plenty of extra background white space to ensure that the background colour doesn't peek through.

The main advantage is that it allow icons to be reusable, so instead of needing three images for default, hover and active states, we'll only need one.

Pure CSS icons

Can we make an icon out of just CSS? It turns out we can! Lucian Marin has developed a way of creating icons using a combination of markup and CSS. CSS icons can scale, plus it's easy to change the icon's colour with just a little extra CSS.

Here's the markup for Lucian's clock icon:

```
<div class="icon icon-clock">
  <div class="icon-clock-circle"></div>
  <div class="icon-clock-line-1"></div>
  <div class="icon-clock-line-2"></div>
  <span class="name">Clock</span>
</div>
```

Of course, we can choose other elements if they are more appropriate to the meaning of our content. Now let's build Lucian's clock using CSS. First, the outer icon division. We'll give it dimensions and some margins, plus we'll apply position: relative; to make it a positioning context for it's positioned child elements.

```
.icon {
  position: relative;
  width:16px;
  height:16px;
  margin: 16px;
}
```

Now let's create that clock face. We'll give it a black border and round the element to a circle by applying a border-radius that's 50% of it's size. We'll also position this circle absolutely inside our icon container.

```css
.icon-clock-circle {
  border-color: #000;
  border-style: solid;
  border-width: 2px;
  border-radius:50%;
  width: 12px;
  height: 12px;
  position: absolute;
  top:0;
  left:0;
}
```

Finally, we'll create the two black clock hands and position them both inside our clock face.

```css
.icon-clock-line-1 {
  background-color: #000;
  width: 1px;
  height: 6px;
  position: absolute;
  top:3px;
  left:7px;
}
```

```css
.icon-clock-line-2 {
  background-color: #000;
  width: 4px;
  height: 1px;
  position: absolute;
  top:8px;
  left:8px;
}
```

I interviewed Lucian to find out more about this technique.

Peculiar icons

Peculiar

Peculiar is a free icon package made only in CSS. It was created for sites and web applications that depend on fewer HTTP requests as possible or don't need to use any image at all. The package contains 45 pictograms that are available in 16^2 pixels size. More icons are about to come in the future.

Download — contains the HTML & CSS files with the needed code

Donate — donations are greatly appreciated

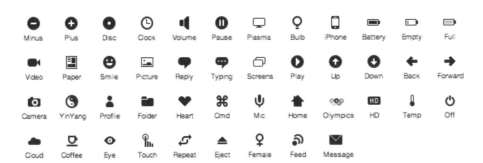

Minus	Plus	Disc	Clock	Volume	Pause	Plasma	Bulb	iPhone	Battery	Empty	Full
Video	Paper	Smile	Picture	Reply	Typing	Screens	Play	Up	Down	Back	Forward
Camera	YinYang	Profile	Folder	Heart	Cmd	Mic	Home	Olympics	HD	Temp	Off
Cloud	Coffee	Eye	Touch	Repeat	Eject	Female	Feed	Message			

Endless possibilities are coming with these type of icons. Sizes are not limited to 16^2 pixels,

How did Peculiar come about?

" I created Peculiar because I was frustrated with the usual workflow of making little changes to graphics on web interfaces. You usually have to go back and forth between a coding application, FTP application and an image editing application just for making small changes like colour, transparency, adding white space where it's needed, and so on. All this can be avoided using only CSS and by changing a few lines of code. Using CSS icons you can do multiple colour themes for a site without having to manage tens or hundreds of small graphics files.

When zooming the page, some of the icons break up — is this solvable?

" The scaling of CSS icons is the same problem Apple faced when they multiplied the resolution of the iPhone by two. This is more of a browser and OS problem: they have to do some sort of sub-pixel scaling for CSS elements (borders, widths, heights, margins, radius) to look good between 100% and 200% scaling. And even if they do this, they will look blurry. I attached an image with Peculiar zoomed at 200% and you can see it is pixel-perfect. I avoid the problem by making bigger versions of the icons at 32×32 pixels or 64×64 pixels.

How long does it take you (on average) to create each one?

" I created the whole set in 7–9 days. It took me 2–3 hours for creating the very first CSS icons and mastering the technique. Then it was more of a talent and inspiration problem. I didn't use any CSS transformations (rotate), so I had to choose icons that have basic shapes like rectangles, squares, triangles and circles. This was because IE9 doesn't support CSS transforms.

So, what are the advantages of pure CSS icons?

- No images or fonts to download, just a style sheet.
- Icons can scale infinitely, at least in theory.
- Unlike using an icon font, there is no meaningless content in the markup, and there is scope to have different colours within the icon.

And the disadvantages?

- Scaling isn't perfect, and icons will break at odd-numbered zoom percentages.
- Markup can often include purely presentational elements.
- Designing new icons can be time-consuming compared with creating vector artwork.
- Limited support for CSS transforms in less capable browsers limits how complex our shapes can be.

I believe that the advantages of CSS icons make them worthy of discussion in this book but, for me, the disadvantages of uneven scaling and longer production time mean that I wouldn't use them right now. However, for occasions when you only need one or two icons, they could be worth considering. The technique has a lot of potential and is bound to improve in the future.

Summary

For high-traffic sites or large amounts of icons, sprites still make the most sense. There are instances where low volume makes delivery systems such as fonts a possibility, though, and these methods are only going to get better.

My personal hope for the future is a combination of sprites in conjunction with a vector format like SVG or Raphaël that also allows objects to have their own IDs. Everything in one document, in a scalable format, that also allows for reuse with interchangeable colours, no screen reader problems or fiddling about with `background-position`.

One day...

Chapter references

Mac OS X Developer Library - Using Tiff Utility
http://developer.apple.com/library/mac/#DOCUMENTATION/Darwin/Reference/ManPages/man1/tiffutil.1.html

IconBuilder
http://iconfactory.com/software/iconbuilder

MultiTiff
http://www.literatureandlatte.com/freestuff/index.html

Raphaël Library
http://raphaeljs.com/

Helvetireader
http://helvetireader.com/

Web Semantics Data URI Convertor
http://websemantics.co.uk/online_tools/image_to_data_uri_convertor/

HTML5 Custom Data Attributes
http://html5doctor.com/html5-custom-data-attributes/

Further Reading

Resolution Independent Fever
http://www.red-sweater.com/blog/223/resolution-independent-fever

Iconfactory: Resolution Independence for Developers
http://iconfactory.com/home/permalink/1731

Data Attributes: Blurring the Line Between Content and Presentation?

http://chriseppstein.github.com/blog/2010/09/01/blurring-the-line-between-content-and-presentation-with-data-attributes/

Becoming a Font Embedding Master

http://snook.ca/archives/html_and_css/becoming-a-font-embedding-master

Font-Embedding Icons: This Is a Big Deal

http://somerandomdude.com/articles/design-technology/font-embedding-icons/

Ever Thought About Using @Font-face for Icons?

http://net.tutsplus.com/tutorials/html-css-techniques/quick-tip-ever-thought-about-using-font-face-for-icons/

The Making of GUI Design Icons Font:

http://vector.tutsplus.com/articles/case-study/the-making-of-gui-design-icons-font/

HTML5 Data Attribute

http://html5doctor.com/html5-custom-data-attributes/

Selectivizr

http://selectivizr.com/

CSS3 Image Masks

http://developer.apple.com/library/safari/#documentation/InternetWeb/Conceptual/SafariVisualEffectsProgGuide/Masks/Masks.html

CSS Inline Images and the Data URI

http://www.7cynics.com/webdesign/css/css-inline-images-data-uri.html

How to draw with HTML5 canvas

http://thinkvitamin.com/code/how-to-draw-with-html-5-canvas/
http://dev.opera.com/articles/view/html-5-canvas-the-basics/

Chapter 7

Application icons

We've developed our icon skills throughout this book, thinking about how we use icons and where they came from, then looking at designing simple favicons. We followed this up by tackling metaphors, pictograms and small colour icons. In this chapter, we'll round off the book by exploring in detail the most complex and independent icon form: application icons.

Until 2001, both Windows 2000 and Mac OS 9 gave you just a 32px square in which to represent an application. The release of Windows XP pushed this to 48px, but the introduction of Mac OS X marked a leap to a whopping (at the time) 128px. The larger canvas allowed more opportunity for expression, as well as detail, and application icons became more like photorealistic illustrations. I make no apologies for the heavy Mac OS X bias in this chapter — the majority of the best application icons are to be found on that platform — but the aspects covered in the examples could be applied anywhere.

The Mac OS X icons also revisited the office metaphor, but developed it further. It's main application icons were designed to have the same perspective as if viewed on a desk in front of you, while utility applications had icons that were seen as more serious, with more muted colours and a face-on perspective.

Apple's Address Book (left) and TextEdit (right) follow the desktop perspective, while apps like Podcast Capture (centre) are utilities and are viewed face-on

Windows icons, in comparison, show a lower angle and from more to one side

At the time of writing, the largest supported icon size is a whopping (really this time) 1,024×1,024px, on Mac OS X 10.7 (Lion). It's believed that this size has been created in readiness for higher density screens in the future as it's not currently used anywhere in the interface. Regardless of the use case, it can always be useful to have a large, high-res version of the icon available for other purposes. While the cost of developing a high-res icon would have been laughable in the past, other possible uses (such as website, merchandising and promotional material) make it a good investment.

David Lanham's icon for TextMate 2 (left)

Apple´s preview

While this chapter deals mostly with the desktop, the context for application icons has also grown to include mobile too: Android and iOS in particular. While Android allows and indeed encourages application icons with unique outlines, iOS restricts these to a rounded square. Some artists have found ways to make the best of this, such as the Camera Genius app designed by Artua (right) and TapDJ (below). By cleverly using the corner radius as part of the image, you're less aware of it, and it feels more like a desktop application icon.

Many of the drawing techniques covered in Chapter 5 apply to application icons as well, but there is the added complexity of realism to add to those skills. Rather than show step-by-step tutorials as I did in Chapter 5, which would become rather tedious, I want to showcase icon artists' different workflows, and how they portray different materials, lighting effects and surfaces. There are also three main areas where application icons differ to the other types of icon covered so far: resolutions, metaphor and process.

Resolutions

Application icons usually contain multiple sizes of bitmaps (called resources) in a single container file: for Windows, this is in the form of an ICO file; for Mac OS X it's an ICNS. On the other hand, Modern Linux distributions — such as Ubuntu — use a folder of separate SVG files for each resource.

The possible sizes required can be confusing, but not all sizes are needed, depending on the context:

Version	Format	16px	22px	24px	32px	48px	64px	96px	128px	256px	512px	1024px
LINUX (UBUNTU HUMANITY SET)												
	.svg	●	●	●	●	●	●		●			
MAC OS X												
10.0 - .4	.icns	●			●				●			
10.5 - .6		●			●				●	●	●	
10.7		●			●				●	●	●	○
WINDOWS												
95 - 2000	.ico	●		●	●	●						
XP		●		●	●	●				●		
Vista / Windows 7		●			●	●		○		●		

○ = Supported, but optional

The larger sizes also allow the opportunity for easter eggs — little treats for those who go looking for them, like this special message in the icon for CSS Edit:

In addition to ICOand ICNS, there is a third called iContainer, developed by Panic Software, created to package sets of Mac icons. It supports icons up to 512px and includes display settings and information about each icon. It is primarily used in Panic's CandyBar app for organising icons and customising Mac OS X system and application icons.

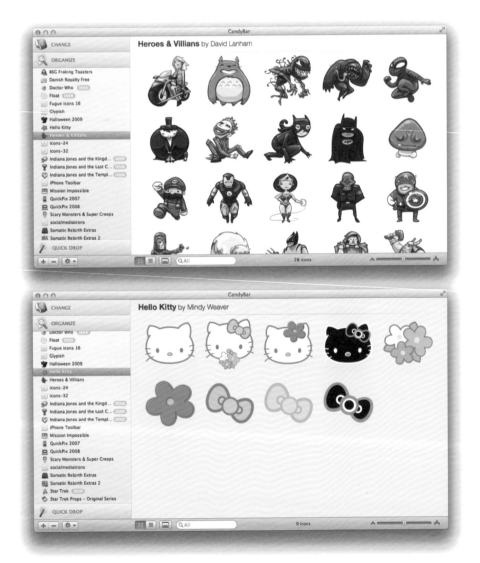

The iContainer format contains a set of icons, including information like the title and designer, and even the colour of background they should be displayed on in apps like CandyBar

This format is also supported by Opacity (which can export and import a set of icons as an iContainer), LiteIcon and Axialis IconWorkshop (see the appendix). In a similar way, Windows supports icon library (.icl) for packaging multiple icons in one file.

LittleSnapper icon (Bartelme Design)

I've been following the work of Austrian Wolfgang Bartelme for many years now. He's created many of the icons for apps that I use every day at Hicksdesign and, in particular, RealMac Software's Littlesnapper.

What was your starting point in icon design? What turned you on to it and what were your inspirations?

I did my first icons more than ten years ago during my studies of information design. It was the early days of Windows XP and Mac OS X and I was excited about their fresh new look. I admired the icons of Windows XP because of their simplicity and consistency, and loved the ones from Mac OS X because of their attention to detail. However, the thing that really made me want to do icons was the fact that they've become much more than just simple representations of an app. Now they've become its face, its personality. I loved that and wanted to do similar. I started to release my own free icons on my website. People seemed to like them and I soon got my first contract work.

What tools do you use to design icons, beside sketching?

I use both Illustrator and Photoshop to draw icons. I tend to start in Illustrator — basic shapes and shading — and then continue in Photoshop for the finishing touches.

Can you tell me about the design process for the LittleSnapper icon? How did you get the idea and what other approaches did you try and discount?

I really enjoyed working on the LittleSnapper icon. Not just because I liked the concept of the app, but also because I could immediately picture the final app icon. It was clear that I wanted to incorporate some sort of camera or a lens to visualize the whole snapping aspect of the app. In order to convey that the app is about taking screenshots, I added a stylised browser window. I think it turned out pretty nice - definitely one of my favourite projects.

Metaphor

While the metaphor is still important, conventions and all the criteria discussed in Chapter 4 are not. An application icon's function is to be memorable first, and describe or suggest what the tool does second, although the latter is not mandatory. In the case of LittleSnapper, following a similar convention to Apple's iPhoto worked really well as a way of describing it's function. The camera and browser window, overlaid with viewfinder display, depicts taking whole webpages or elements of them. Often a real object is used, something familiar that might also create an emotional response, such as the Espresso icon:

In my opinion, one of the biggest factors that I feel makes a memorable application icon is, quite simply, fun. The visual metaphor for AppZapper, the Mac OS X uninstaller tool, could've been a workmanlike affair but, instead of a literal depiction of an app in a wastebasket, they've gone for a retro-style ray gun, which is far more distinctive.

In the same way, Panic's Transmit icon rejects attempting to depict the potentially dull subject of FTP transfer, choosing a transportation metaphor instead, with it's familiar yellow truck. It's been doing this since Mac OS 9, and has kept up with all the changes in icon resolution, from an original aliased 32px icon, to the current 1,024px masterpiece:

The history of the Transmit icon, from early Mac OS 9 32px versions before the truck metaphor was used (top left) to very latest artwork, a whopping 2,048px!

Taking the concept of fun even further, there is a trend for cute mascots in icon metaphors. The icon for the multi-protocol instant messaging client Adium has three different states: asleep (when the app isn't open); awake; and when a new message arrives, it flaps it's wings:

If you have a family of applications, then you may want to use a common theme to show this. Tapbots make a series of iOS apps (or bots as they prefer to call them) which cleverly use the same robotic eyes to provide the link, sometimes including the interface of the app itself:

An abstract icon can work really well, if it has a distinctive and intriguing form like Realmac Software's Analog, based on the shape of a camera shutter.

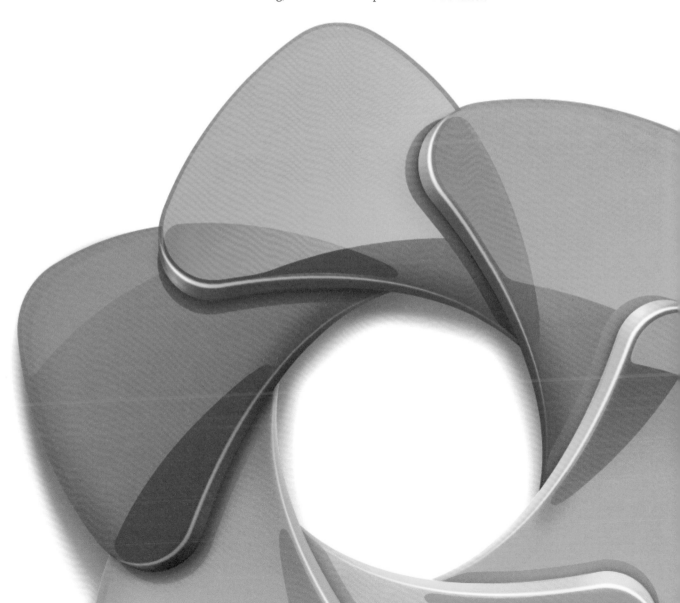

Process

The process for creating application icons will vary, but there are three stages that are prevalent in many designers' workflows.

Sketching

I've already banged on about this in Chapter 5, but pencil sketching is a great way to try out lots of different ideas and variations of viewing angles in a short space of time. Some like to use this stage to try colour sketches too, but generally that's left to the next stage.
It's also a way of becoming familiar with the subject. If it's a real object, you naturally distil it down to its important features by sketching it. If you're creating a character, like the Adium duck, then sketching it gets you used to its form, and enables you to draw it consistently from other angles. This is something I found particularly valuable when making the Silverback icon; it required a lot of sketching before I became confident I knew how to draw a gorilla.

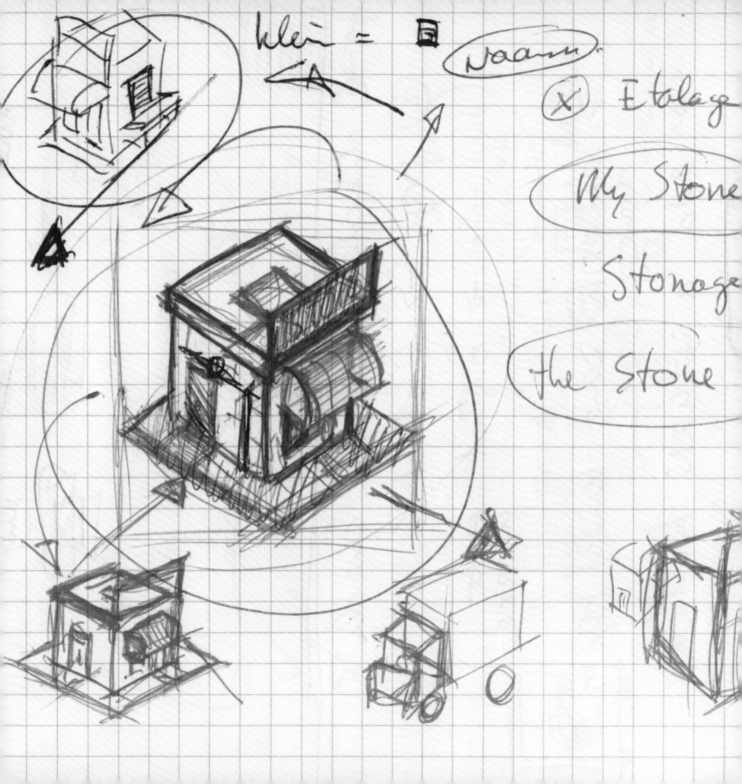

klein = 🔲

Naam

ⓧ Etalage

My Store

Storage

The Store

Vector sketch

Once you become used to vector editors, it's possible to create simple test illustrations to see how an icon could work. Without showing detail, the basic shapes are drawn out and, with simple gradients, the concept can be demonstrated. While, at first glance, the gradients may make them appear quite involved, in fact they can be put together pretty quickly. At this stage, you're not taking into account considerations such as sizing elements correctly for scaling, and it provides a good visual for the client to judge. These are usually drawn on top of scanned-in pencil sketches and can often become the basis of the final rendering.

Below are David Lanham's original vector sketches for the Coda icon, before the idea of the distinctive leaf was used:

We will look at the Coda icon in more detail, later in this chapter.

Drawing and iteration

Once the client has approved the icon design direction, the detailed work begins.

Whenever I create icons, it's always with the final output method in mind and, in the case of application icons, I use IconBuilder to create the final ICO and ICNS files. Rather than forcing you to use a drawing editor that you're unfamiliar with, IconBuilder is a plugin for Photoshop and Fireworks that allows you to export your artwork to icon resource files, as well as multiple bitmap formats (including multipage TIFFs — see Chapter 6). Even though I work predominantly in Adobe Illustrator, I always import my final .ai artwork into Photoshop to use IconBuilder for the final part of the process.

IconBuilder comes with Photoshop templates for laying out your various resources in a preset grid, so that it knows where to find them when it comes to building the icon files.

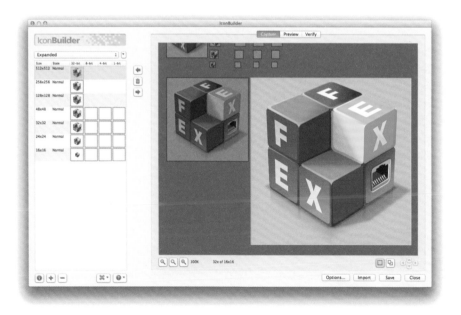

You can create your own grids and presets too: for example, ones for creating favicons and Apple Touch icons. I have one set up in Illustrator that mimics the preset Photoshop template, so that when I import the artwork the resources are in the correct place to build.

More on this part of the process at the end, but it's worth mentioning now as it affects how we lay out our resources. There are other export options, too, listed in the appendix, but believe me when I say that IconBuilder is the daddy.

The exceptions to this are graphic editors such as Opacity (Mac) or Axialis IconWorkshop (Windows), which can not only create icons but also export directly to both of the required icon formats (as well as bitmaps).

So, with a grid ready, the starting point is almost always the largest icon. In fact, designers like Kenichi Yoshida from Panic Software start with a canvas twice the largest supported size. That now means a really, really whopping great big 2,048px square. By doing this, you not only have a good quality large version for other purposes, but it also helps construct the detail. For me, the added benefit is that any imperfections become invisible once reduced down, but it does, of course, mean a lot more maths when working out how it's going to scale!

This is the stage that varies the most among artists — most prefer Photoshop, with Illustrator second, and a growing number now like to render in a 3-D modelling package such as Cinema 4D or Maya. This allows different perspectives and light sources to be explored. If a client decides they would prefer to portray the object from a different angle, it can be done without having to redraw from scratch.

One icon created in this way is Sofa's Checkout, seen here in three stages. First, the wireframe rendering, where the object is described only by lines. Then, the ambient occlusion render, where the effect of light direction on the surfaces and their textures are drawn. The final version shows the details added at the Photoshop stage.

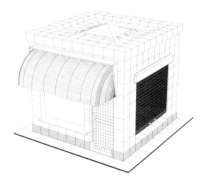

3-D wireframe render

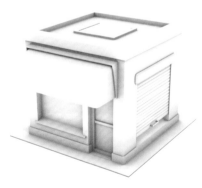

3-D Ambient Occlusion render

Final icon resources for Checkout app

Jono Hunt (Iconaholic)

To see what process other icon artists use, I talked to many other designers, including fellow Brit Jono Hunt (better known as Iconaholic), a specialist in icon and UI design. His icon for Radioline, 'the missing radio app for the Mac', hit all the right notes with my love for retro objects.

What is your process for creating application icons?

I almost always start in Illustrator. If I've found some reference images to look at, I place them in the bottom layer (locked) so that everything is in the same artboard. I turn on the grid and in the view menu I set it to pixel preview and enable snap to pixel.

When creating icons at different perspectives, I often use the basic 3-D tools in Illustrator to get the angle and perspective looking right. They're not great for anything advanced, but do help when starting work on an icon to get the perspective looking correct. Once I'm happy, I'll expand the shape and continue working with it, adding colours, highlights, and so on. Once you've expanded a 3-D object in Illustrator, it usually adds lots of points to the shapes which seems pretty messy. In the past I would often leave the shapes with all the messy points, but lately I use a tool from the VectorScribe plug-in called 'smart remove point and close path' (from the plug-in's PathScribe palette). It's really easy to select and remove all those points while keeping the original shape intact to clean up the objects.

I make the basic shapes with flat contrasting colours so that they're easy to distinguish while arranging them. Once the icon starts to resemble the image I have of it in my head, I start adding the intended colours, highlights and shadows.

I often duplicate the icon, making changes and comparing the old and new versions side by side to see which works best. I keep on duplicating them throughout the process, comparing different variations all the time. Once I'm getting to the point where I've made all of the shapes, added some colours and effects and it's looking like something I'm happy with (probably about 80% completed), I save it as a new Illustrator document and delete all the old versions so that I just have one version to continue with. I'll then carry on tweaking, trying different colours, sizes of objects and such like.

I often add shadows and other effects to the larger sizes in Illustrator, but it doesn't handle blur, inner glow and some others well at smaller sizes (usually below 128px). If this is the case, I then switch to Photoshop to tweak them and finish them off there.

If I'm creating something quite realistic, I tend to look at a lot of photos of the objects and how the light falls on them. I sometimes sample the colours directly from example photos I'm using for reference. With the Radioline icon, I wanted the radio to be plastic but not really glossy like a lot of Mac icons. I wanted it to look quite retro and not too over the top.

How do you arrive at the final idea?

" Sometimes the client will already have an idea of how they want it to look, but more often than not I'll take a look at the app and what it does, and then have a look for metaphors and reference on iStockphoto, Google images and Wikipedia. After getting some ideas, I'll send the suggestions to the client and we'll discuss which ones they like and what ideas could work best until we're both happy with the decision (or occasionally until the client says 'No, go with the other idea. The one you don't like.' o_o).

Original sketch and final icon for Permute

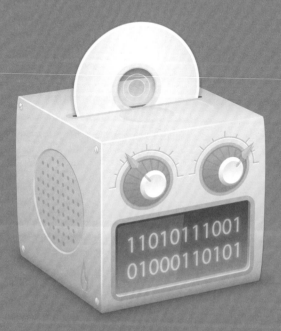

In the case of the Permute icon, once I learned what the app would do, I had an idea for some kind of box. Like a jack-in-the-box or music box, with a handle on the side to turn or wind up. Put some media in the top, turn the handle and the converted version comes out of the front. The client liked the general idea but wanted some changes. He wanted a CD or DVD in the top where I'd suggested a film strip and some musical notes. He didn't want the handle on the side and wanted to show a screen on the front with binary.

I don't always sketch ideas for clients, especially if the metaphor being described is easily understandable, but I do for some of the crazier ideas that aren't easy for people to visualise. I did a quick sketch of the Permute icon and found it (unintentionally) resembled a robot's head, with the two dials at the top (eyes) and the screen at the bottom (mouth). I quite liked it, so I sent the sketch to the client pointing out that if he didn't like that idea then I could switch the dials to the bottom and the screen to the top to prevent that. I'd originally planned to make the box wooden so, hopefully, it wouldn't have been a problem. He liked the idea so we went with it.

What tools do you prefer and why?

I mainly use Illustrator and Photoshop along with IconBuilder, the Photoshop plug-in, to build the final icon files.

Even if I'm going to work on an icon in Photoshop, I'll often create the basic shapes in Illustrator, then copy and paste them into Photoshop to continue. I guess I feel more comfortable with it and like to use the space of the artboard and spread everything out in there.

I tend to use Photoshop for smaller icons and UI work. Also, Photoshop seems better for adding effects such as blur, inner glow and so on at smaller sizes, and when using textures.

What is your strategy for creating the various sizes required for the icon file?

" *I'll make the larger sizes first and then resize them down for the smaller sizes. I turn on the grid and in the view menu I set it to pixel preview (Illustrator) and enable snap to pixel. I check each size and make sure the pixels are aligned and snapped to the grid, tweak the layer styles (Photoshop) or effects (Illustrator), and remove some of the details for the smaller sizes. For 32px and 16px sizes, the icons are usually simpler versions of the larger sizes and I'll remake them completely.*

Is your process for other icons (such as toolbars) any different?

" *If I'm creating thirty toolbar icons, I'll make them all in the same Illustrator document. If I'm making smaller icons in Photoshop, I tend to create one document for each icon, unless they're variations of the same icon. I'm not too sure why I work one way with Illustrator and another way with Photoshop. I'm just comfortable working like this.*

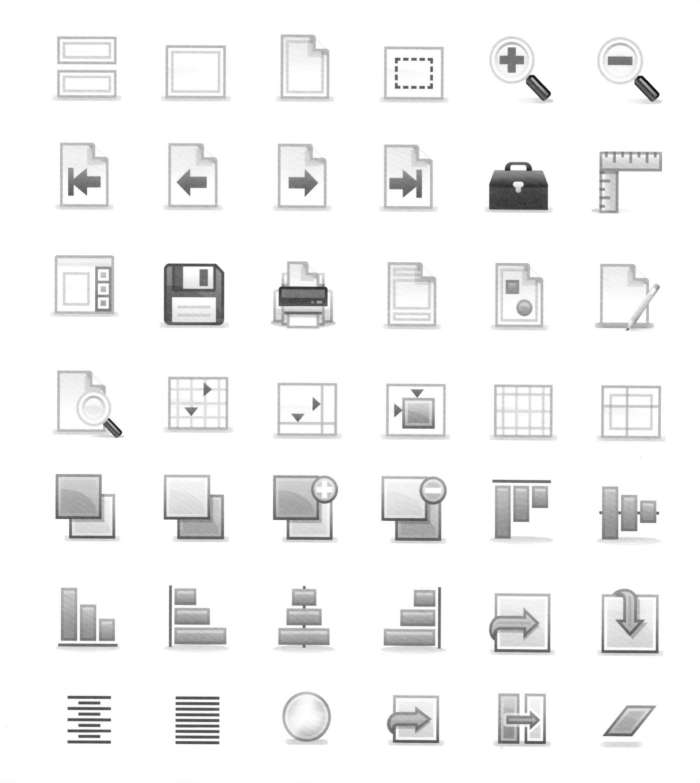

Realism

Just as with the colour icons covered in Chapter 5, light direction is the first point to consider, as this will affect the shading. However, there are more complications with application icons. With smaller colour icons, any shadows could be done quickly and effectively with just transparent black, but here we need to be more lifelike. Realistic shadows are either warm (hint of red) or cold (hint of blue), and this can be used to suggest temperature as well as feeling more natural.

This is something you would notice on white areas the most, and shading can change the subconscious impression made by the icon. For example, the shading on a white lab coat may look better being on the colder spectrum, as this would suggest sterility and cleanliness. Warmer shading makes sense on natural white objects such as chalk or a polar bear. The same methodology can be applied to grey colours, too. Straight grey can be dull, whereas a warm or cool grey will appear more natural.

Things (left) uses cool shading, while the Oxley letter (right) uses warm shading. Oxley letter by the Iconfactory, from Indiana Jones and the Kingdom of the Crystal Skull™ © 2008 Lucasfilm Ltd

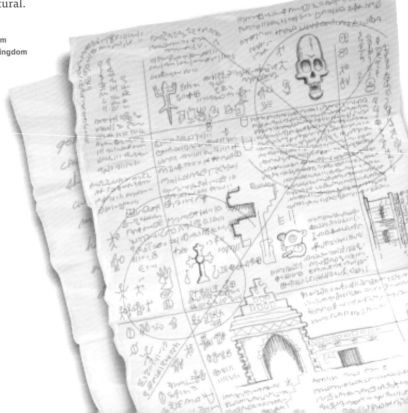

Light direction, highlights and shading are also how you describe the surface of the object. I mentioned before that the light source doesn't always come from above: in this jack-o'-lantern, the main light source comes from inside.

Jack-o'-lantern icon by the Iconfactory

The gloss finish of the Unison app's magnet creates sharp highlights and reflects other elements, even in the shadows.

Objects with glass or transparent plastic also create a challenge with reflections. The slide ring on the icon for Carousel manages to show not only warped internal reflections but also a clear light source on top.

Surfaces may also have a texture that will change depending on the light. As well as making the highlights and shadows softer, it will create patterns. Going back to the Camera Genius icon, there are three main textures to highlight:

Faux-leather grip uses a pattern with both highlight and shadow. Notice how the highlights become stronger nearer the top

Black plastic is a much subtler texture, best recreated with something like a noise filter

Brushed metal is suggested with soft, slightly darker, horizontal lines

The other element to consider is perspective, and there are three possible kinds. One point perspective has just one vanishing point (as in Carousel), but you may need two or three vanishing points, depending on what you need to show.

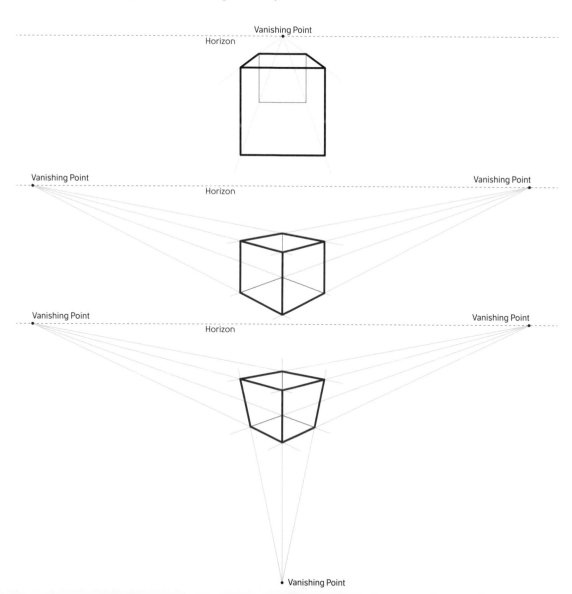

Your graphics app may contain tools for creating and drawing on a perspective grid, but you can make a basic one yourself easily enough with guides. This is another area where artists are using 3-D rendering applications instead of traditional 2-D tools because, once built, the perspective can be tweaked easily to find the view that looks right.

It takes many years of experience and observation to be able to draw realistic imagery solely from memory but, as we use metaphors for application icons (such as the leaf for Coda), it's possible to get the best reference possible — the object itself. We can get a lot of good reference material from sources like stock libraries and Google image searches, but having the object in front of you means that you can control the lighting and perspective. You may also discover detail and nuances you might not have seen in a flat photo, elements that will be useful for creating the larger sizes of the icon.

If it's not possible or practical to do this, another option is to make a rough model that allows us to study its form. When creating the abstract icon for Kaleidoscope, Jasper Hauser used plasticine to mock up the sketches he had made (see the Kaleidoscope case study later on).

Application icon process —

drawing inspiration from others

To go into the process in more detail, I've chosen my favourite examples of application icons and talked to the designers in question to see how they made them, and what tools, methods and approaches they use generally in their icon work.

CSS3 Toolkit icon by Cian Walsh. View Cian's process here http://afterglow.ie/design_interface.html

Coda icon

When I first decided to write a book about icon design,
I knew there was one icon in particular that I wanted
to feature — my favourite application icon (and
indeed a favourite application as well): David
Lanham's sumptuous work for Panic Software's
Coda. I talked to David about the process and
iterations for creating the Coda icon, as well
as his icon work in general.

The latest version of the Coda icon is by Kenichi Yoshida

What tools do you use to design icons beside sketching?

The sketch pad is definitely my favourite tool, but a lot of time is also spent researching the subject matter and gathering references to do the sketches from. I've found that actually seeing an object in person or taking reference photos yourself immensely helps in understanding the materials and other qualities of what you're trying to draw. I was struggling with drawing a hammer once, but one quick trip to the hardware store to check out all the various styles, materials and types of hammers, and the results instantly showed up when I went to redraw the icon. Internet searches can work, but there's nothing like first-hand experience to help you understand what you'll be rendering out.

You're known as an illustrator, rather than specifically an icon designer. Do you find any difference in workflow to how you approach an illustration and an icon?

My approach to drawing an icon versus an illustration is pretty close to being the same. The initial steps of research, brainstorming and sketching all apply, the subtle difference being that I have to keep in mind how the final drawing will be used. Icons generally need transparent backgrounds and easily recognisable shapes and colours that work on a variety of backgrounds; illustrations need more focus on composition and colour relationships. They both need to get the message across quickly and efficiently, however, and with icon sizes getting larger and larger, they're becoming more about illustration than ever before.

Your style encompasses both highly photorealistic icons like Coda, but also a more illustrative style, especially with character designs like those in the game Ramp Champ. Do you have preference?

" I fully enjoy both styles; they play against each other really well with one being very tight and planned, the other being very loose and freeform. Given the choice, I'd lean toward the illustrative style in a heartbeat; I absolutely love drawing characters and letting the drawing lead me to the final result rather than having to plan things beforehand. A lot of my icon design starts off very loose (it's great for brainstorming exercises), and I try to let as much of that make its way to the final icon as I can, since I love the spontaneity in the drawings.

How did the idea of the Coda icon come about? Did you explore many other ideas, or was it always going to be a leaf from the start?

" The icon began as a group effort among the Iconfactory employees and many of the initial sketches were based on construction and machinery metaphors. There were welding masks, construction hats, a forklift and various directions like that. However, we quickly realised that most of these directions felt terribly outdated and lacked any emotional aspects for such a fun and new piece of software. So we changed our approach to focus on the potential for creation that the software enables. Among the new ideas were, of course, the leaf, an acorn and a sprouting seed. I think this was just around the time that the drawing software Acorn was showing up, so we cut that one and ended up on the leaf for its direct simplicity and shape.

There were many iterations of the icon, playing with different shading and details before the icon was finalised

Did it take many iterations to get right?

" The overall shape and color didn't take long at all, but the shading got tricky. I was working too large and focusing on details for the first round and lost sight of what it would look like scaled down, so the initial pass was way too bulky once we tried it out. The next iteration improved on this with redrawn veins and shadows where the top section of the leaf was darker and the bottom caught the light but, again, when scaled down it was too drastic a difference. So I knocked that back and it instantly improved the feel, but the veins seemed too prominent and the yellow tones in the veins kept the leaf from feeling fresh and lush. Once the veins were flipped to dark, everyone was very happy with the results and it was down to a matter of minor refinements like smoothing out the edges of the leaf and cleaning up the smaller sizes of the icon.

How do you approach the task of creating the various resolutions? Do you start with a particular size first?

" If there are critical details that need to be preserved, then I try to either draw it on a proportional grid (so a 1px drop of water in the 32px size is the correct size in the 512px drawing), or draw a basic icon at 32px and use that for a template for the larger sizes. Lately, I've been creating icons at 2,048px and larger to future-proof everything, so figuring out those proportional requirements has been really important. Smart objects in Photoshop also help immensely with this. I create them for all the key sizes and, as I update the large master file, I can instantly see the results throughout the sizes. No matter what, there is always manual clean-up needed with the pencil tool for small sizes, but any chance to minimise that need is always helpful. Occasionally, icons just don't scale acceptably and need complete redrawing for small sizes like the 32px and 16px resources.

Which icon project have you enjoyed the most?

" All the organic icons I've drawn like the Coda leaf, the bee for On the Job, or the Twitterrific bird, I've thoroughly enjoyed. Nature provides an infinite amount of detail to reference and extracting what's important to include or exclude in the rendering is like a mini game during the entire process.

Windows Vista icons

Gedeon Maheux, The Iconfactory

It would be impossible to write a book about icons without featuring the Iconfactory, founded in 1996 by Corey Marion, Talos Tsui and Gedeon Maheux. While it's a software and design company, well known for creating its own apps and games, the team has created many well-known icons, as well as giving away fun high-quality icons to beautify your desktops. It was also the work of the Iconfactory that inspired me to start creating my own icons.

They've worked on many different jobs, ranging from small projects to quite possibly the largest icon project imaginable: Microsoft Vista.

What was your starting point in icon design? What turned you on to it and what were your inspirations?

My first job was actually as a multimedia designer creating educational CD-ROMs for kids. Part of that job was to design the 32px icons that were to be used on the CD-ROMs themselves in the directory structure. This was back in the days of Mac System 7 and OS 8 when we only had a limited canvas size and color palette from which to draw on.

I discovered quickly that I enjoyed pushing pixels into small works of art and took it up as a hobby. I didn't make a living at it until quite some time later when I started doing icon design as freelance work on the side. Some of the first professional paid icon projects I worked on were Outlook Express for the Mac and the Keychain Access suite from Apple.

What tools do you use to design icons besides sketching?

Of course, the tools have evolved over the years from placing pixels in simple programs like ResEdit and then in Adobe Photoshop, to vector-based tools like the now defunct Macromedia Freehand. Today, I do my icon creation almost exclusively in Photoshop with vector shapes and layer effects. I still use Adobe Illustrator for some work, but I've been trying to keep myself from doing that when I can, since Illustrator can be somewhat imprecise. From there, I use the Iconfactory's own IconBuilder plug-in for Photoshop to build the actual resources for the desktop. I organise and sort all of my final icons in CandyBar, another Iconfactory/Panic product, for handy reference.

search

notepad

paint

networked object

recycle bin

Early sketches for the Vista icon set

Creating the icon set for Windows Vista and 7 must've been an immense task. Did you do them all yourself or was a team involved?

" Oh, no. I was only one member of the team and when I say team I mean that, because both of these suites of icons were a total team effort spanning months, sometimes years of work. It was a group effort of the highest order and some of the most demanding work we've ever done as a company.

How did you maintain consistency with the team?

" We had reviews of all work about twice a week internally and once a week with Microsoft. There was a tight focus on a unified look that had to be maintained. Over time, we got quite good at spotting when something didn't quite belong in the suite and correcting accordingly.

I'd love to know what the workflow was that you used with Microsoft. Did you have set stages of feedback and approval? Did they see sketches or finished icons?

" Both Whistler (XP) and Longhorn (Vista) were broken out into milestones of several phases each. Initially, Microsoft broke the entire suites up into chunks of about fifty icons that they wanted in each chunk. These were prioritised so that the most crucial ones (the ones that were seen in the most places) fell first and were to be completed ahead of the others. These core icons would set the style for the rest of the OS and needed to be pixel-perfect in every way.

For Whistler, the sketch phases lasted three to four months and ranged from rough paper sketches to rough vector comps, and then even to tight comps while still all being considered sketches. Many of these initial tight comps never saw the light of day. For the curious, here you can see one of the near-final XP look-and-feels that was abandoned. They saw every stage of development all the way from rough sketch to final rendered icon and had input into all of it. The demands were exacting, which is what you would expect, since Windows is still, to this day, the most seen and used operating system on the planet.

How do you approach the task of creating the various resolutions? Do you start with a particular size first?

" These days, we start with the largest size and scale down. When we do so, we remove detail until it is properly simplified for the correct size it will be shown at. I personally find it much easier to take bits away than to add them, so we prefer to do the bulk of the work upfront and then the scaling portion is usually easier. This also allows the client to see the large, final art and approve that first.

Previously, Windows icons had always been drawn at a particular angle — viewed from the left. Was there a reason to change this perspective with Vista?

" The angle of the icons themselves was dictated by the design of the operating system and throughout 90% of the time we worked on the suite they were in fact drawn from the left. Microsoft only made the perspective change right at the very, very end of Vista's development. Needless to say, this caused a great deal of stress on our part because the entire suite hadn't been drawn to be shown that way. You can read an interesting post about this very subject here:

http://www.istartedsomething.com/20080612/are-windows-vista-icons-facing-the-wrong-way/

How long did the project take to finish?

" Whistler (XP) took four months of designing and four months of production on about 120 icons in total. Longhorn (Vista) took two years to complete, with long stretches of inactivity. Strangely enough, there were fewer icons on Vista to design (about 60), but the project took longer because Microsoft wanted it to be visually outstanding in every way possible. The level of detail and review on Vista was unlike anything we've ever done before.

Early renders for the Vista icon set

Interview

Kaleidoscope icon
by *Sofa*

Kaleidoscope is a file comparison app for spotting the differences in text and image files. Before the app was launched, its striking and abstract icon was published as a teaser movie — leaving the public to try and guess what the app actually did. Instead of representing an actual object, it takes a more abstract approach, while still being memorable. I talked to Jasper Hauser, a member of the Sofa team that created the Kaleidoscope icon.

With a name like Kaleidoscope, why didn't you choose to represent that object as the icon?

It did cross our minds and we actually gave it a shot. But a kaleidoscope isn't a very memorable object, it's a long tube, which also isn't suitable for making an icon out of, as it has to use a square canvas as well as possible. But the visuals a kaleidoscope creates are unique. And so that's why we focused on its unique characteristics instead of the object: playful, colourful, triangular, circular.

How did the idea for Kaleidoscope develop?

" *We started research into Kaleidoscope back in the summer of 2008 and serious development started early 2009. As you can see, there were a couple of subjects that already played an important role:*

- *Inspired by the colourful pieces of glass in a kaleidoscope. The overlaying circles of the RGB colour spectrum show a difference area in the middle, resulting in a rounded triangle shape. Incidentally, this became a concealed reference to the mathematic symbol for difference (delta Δ) as we later discovered :)*

- *I have always had an affinity with M C Escher's infinite and impossible designs and so I thought it could perhaps be used to make the object a lot more visually interesting.*

- *Instead of making the logo the main object of the icon, I tried creating a tablet-like object, on which the logo was displayed. This idea was thrown out pretty early on in the process.*

" *What's interesting to me, looking back at this original sketch, is that it contains all the important concepts that ended up being present in the final icon.*

Since the functionality of Kaleidoscope is quite abstract, it had no useful real life equivalent tool or object we could visually refer to, so the only two options we had were to either invent some kind of device to depict, or come up with an abstract logo-type object.

We tried for some time to come up with a kind of device that could represent the application's functionality but, after having tried it every way that made some sort of sense, we ended up collectively deciding it wasn't going to work. Instead, everybody seemed to be charmed by the logo shape from the original sketch. And so we set off to explore turning that abstract logo into an object that would work as an icon in our Docks.

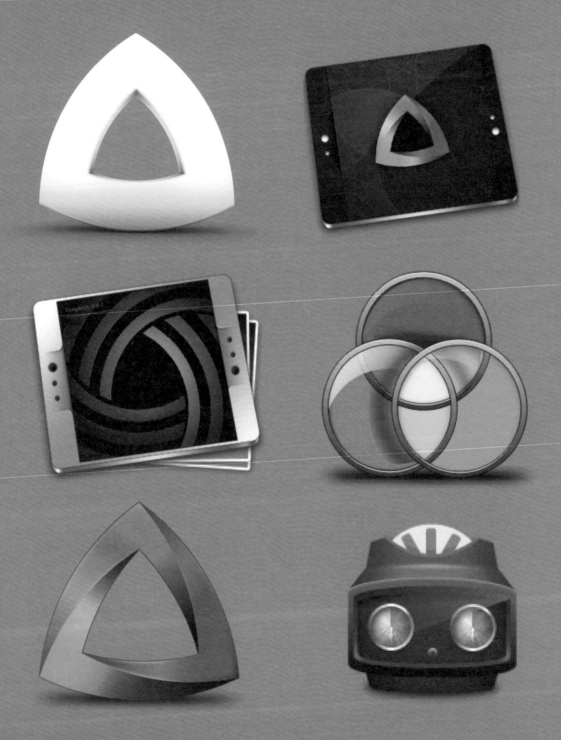

As the story always seems to go when designing a big app icon these days, it required a lot of detail. I couldn't just draw some lines to make up the shape, I had to actually figure out how to accurately build the entire and individual shapes to make it really work.

Additionally, to really get a grip on how the object was constructed and how the shading had to be applied, Hugo van Heuven created a 3-D version of the logo, while I retired to my corner of the office and had a lot of fun using plasticine to try to create my own model of the logo object. But, given the fact that the object has an infinity theme going on and is pretty much an impossible object, depending on your view angle, it wasn't very easy to create the 3-D model.

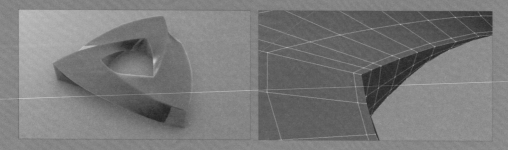

Interestingly, the Kaleidoscope icon has two contrasting features that you see rarely in application icons. The first is its seeming simplicity: it boils down to not much more than an intricate triangle, which greatly helps its recognisability and suitability for use at any scale. Second, it uses every colour imaginable, not something you see often either.

We ended up having an icon pretty early on in the development cycle and so we had plenty of time to take a good look and reflect on it. This is something I really like, mostly because when you are in the creation process you are so deep in the subject matter it becomes progressively more difficult to discern good from bad. The pixel-pushing geeks that we are, we ended up creating several tweaked variations.

The first final iteration was somewhat soft and matte, and so we made it more glossy and aqua looking. As lickable as a Life Saver [author's note to fellow Brits: a brand of American sweets very similar to Polos]. Finally, these changes are very hard to see: it was further cleaned up by making the strokes less heavy, saturating the colors some more, lightening some of the shadows, and simplifying the highlights.

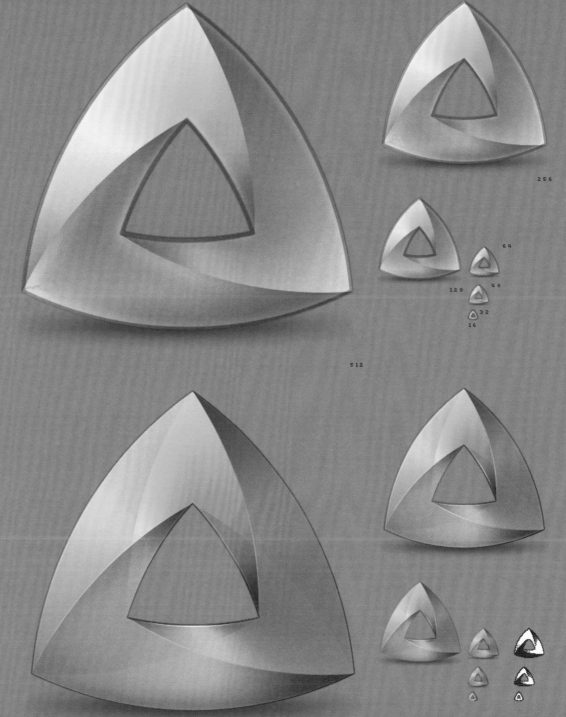

256

512

64

128 48

32

16

Exporting and testing

Unless you're using an app that can export directly to ICO and/or ICNS (Opacity or IconWorkshop — in which case you can skip this step), the artwork now needs to be made into the final icon file and tested. Normally, we would include any context (such as a toolbar background) in the drawing process, but application icons are less predictable and will be viewed on a wide variety of backgrounds. This is particularly the case on recent versions of Windows with the Aero glass theme.

The task of creating the icon formats is most often given to the IconBuilder plugin mentioned at the start of the process. Just as for creating the ICO file for favicons in Chapter 3, with the final artwork on a single layer, the IconBuilder dialog is invoked via the Filters menu. Choose the correct preset for the template you've used, press Build and check each size looks correct in the preview window:

Once you're happy that all the resources are aligned correctly and look spiffing, you can export to multiple formats (ICO, ICNS and bitmaps for each resource) at once.

Alternatively, if you have Apple Developer Tools installed on Mac OS X, you can use the Icon Composer app to import separate bitmaps for each resource, and export as either ICNS or ICO. Unfortunately, it doesn't allow you to add resources for lower colour depths, allocate the 48px icon required for windows, nor a 1,024px for OS X. It works best for quickly creating ICNS files for Mac applications, but is limited compared with IconBuilder.

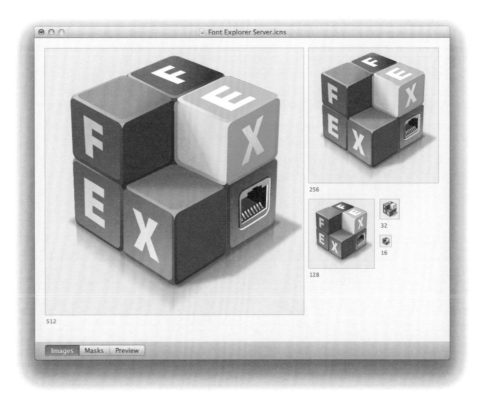

After you've created the icon files, the final stage is to test them. There are various methods for testing and replacing icons without requiring a developer to compile the application.

For testing on Windows, IconBuilder comes with a Windows app, Icontest.exe, for testing the appearance of ICO files. The Mac counterpart, Icon Examiner, will also allow you to view ICO files. Alternatively, folder icons can be changed by right-clicking the relevant folder and and choosing Properties. The Shortcut tab in the Properties window has the option to change the icon through which you can browse and select another ICO file as its replacement.

On Mac OS X, the easiest way to test is to use the icon organisation and customisation software CandyBar to apply new icons. As well as being a tool for collecting and categorising icons, CandyBar allows us to view the different resources via quick look, as well as customising any icon via drag-and-drop. I also use CandyBar as an icon scrapbook where I can study how others have created their icons.

You can also change icons by placing them directly inside the app itself. To look at the ICNS files inside Mac OS X applications, right-click the app, choose Show Package Contents from the context menu, and navigate to Content → Resources where the ICNS is normally stored. The convention is to name the ICNS file with same name as the app (for example, Automator.icns), but sometimes it can be called Appicon.icns, or named after its metaphor (Safari's is compass.icns). These ICNS files can be double-clicked to open by default in Preview, and the individual resources can be dragged-and-dropped from the sidebar to the Finder.

For testing on iOS or Android, we can use the same techniques from Chapter 3 for sites saved as home screen bookmarks. While these contexts can be mocked up, with differences between screens you can't beat viewing them on the actual device.

Summary

I hope you've enjoyed this jaunt through the history, usage and process of making icons. Even if you rarely make anything other than favicons, it has hopefully given you an insight into how icons are made and when (and when not) to use them, which may aid you in other ways, such as general accessibility and usability issues.

This book covers where icon design is right now, but fashions change and the style of icons is always changing with them. At the time of writing, the trend is moving very much towards monochrome pictograms, with application icons being influenced by their simpler mobile app counterparts. I also fully expect to see a reaction against the current high level of photorealism, with more illustrative and creative icon work in the future, and style going beyond merely replicating objects in a lifelike way. I also wonder how long it will be before we start to see animation in application icons, and whether project budgets will increase to cater for the ever larger icon sizes needed.

One thing is for sure, we'll come to a point where talk of needing to keep icons to a pixel grid will disappear. Screens will have higher resolutions and densities to the point where it simply ceases to be an issue.

Until then... keep your pixels crisp!

Chapter references

Kenichi Yoshida
http://www.kenichiyoshida.jp/

VectorScribe Plugin for Illustrator
http://www.astutegraphics.com/products/vectorscribe/

Further reading

History of Windows icons
http://www.windows-icons.com/history.htm

Icon Resource
http://www.iconresource.net/
If you want to delve further in designing application icons, I highly recommend this set of high-quality downloadable PSD and video tutorials by Sebastiaan de With, the fabulous icon designer working for doubleTwist featured in chapter 5's case study.

MadebySofa Blog: Iconic
http://www.madebysofa.com/archive/blog/iconic/
Jasper Hauser tells the story of how the Checkout app icon was created

Appendix

To conclude, I've gathered together various nuggets of useful information as a reference section for the book. Here you will find information on what apps you can use, common badges to add to modify base icons and a comprehensive icon reference chart for looking up the requirements of developing icons for different contexts.

Common icon badges

Badges simply add additional meaning to base icons. For example, to create an add document icon, you could combine a document icon (the base) with the plus sign (modifier). For more explanation on how modifiers can work, see Chapter 4.

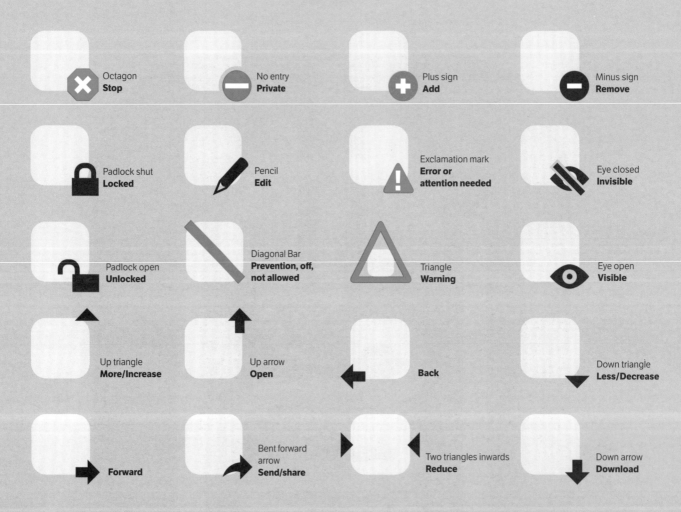

Octagon **Stop**

No entry **Private**

Plus sign **Add**

Minus sign **Remove**

Padlock shut **Locked**

Pencil **Edit**

Exclamation mark **Error or attention needed**

Eye closed **Invisible**

Padlock open **Unlocked**

Diagonal Bar **Prevention, off, not allowed**

Triangle **Warning**

Eye open **Visible**

Up triangle **More/Increase**

Up arrow **Open**

Back

Down triangle **Less/Decrease**

Forward

Bent forward arrow **Send/share**

Two triangles inwards **Reduce**

Down arrow **Download**

Drawing and creation tools

Adobe Illustrator, Photoshop and Fireworks

http://www.adobe.com/products/creativesuite.html
(Mac OS X and Windows)

Without doubt these are the big daddies and should need little introduction or explanation. While Illustrator is biased towards vector tools with some bitmap effects, Photoshop is a bitmap editor with some vector tools, and Fireworks is a mixture of both, but with a focus on web delivery. My personal favourite of all these is Illustrator, although I have been a Fireworks evangelist in the past.

IconBuilder

http://iconfactory.com/software/iconbuilder
(Mac OS X and Windows)

A plug-in for Photoshop and Fireworks that allows you to create icon resource files, as well as multiple bitmap formats (including multipage TIFFs) from your final artwork. If you want to make an icon quickly, there are Photoshop actions for scaling a large image and creating the other resources automatically. It comes with PSD templates and colour swatches to get you started, as well as IconExaminer.app and Icontest.exe, Mac OS X and Windows apps respectively, for viewing icon files.

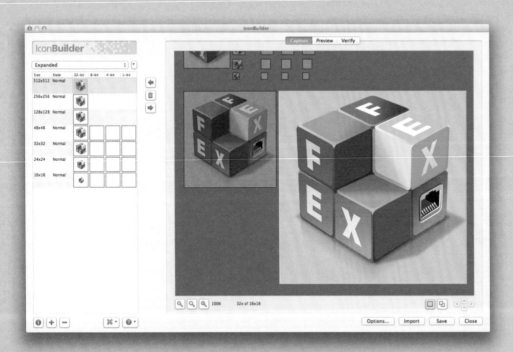

Axialis IconWorkshop

http://www.axialis.com/iconworkshop/

(Windows only)

IconWorkshop is unusual in that it is the only tool created specifically for creating and exporting icons. While it provides its own drawing interface, it supports the import of Photoshop templates. Axialis also provides some excellent tutorial material on creating icons for different contexts: *http://www.axialis.com/ tutorials/index.html*

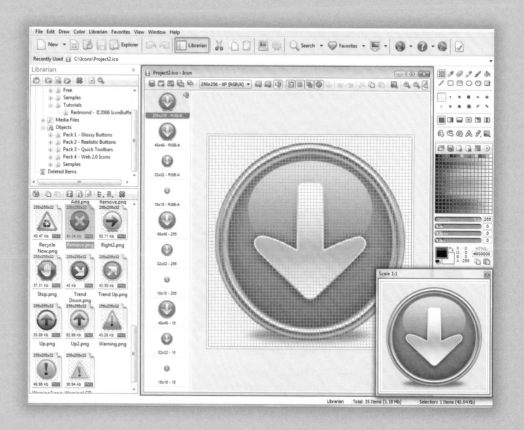

Inkscape

http://inkscape.org/

(Linux, Mac OS X and Windows)

If you prefer your applications to be open source, Inkscape is the only choice of vector editor you'll have. It uses SVG as its native file format but can be very fiddly to use, particularly when trying to draw to pixels. The other option is GIMP, an open source Photoshop alternative, which lacks any vector tools.

Supported Linux distributions are:

- Fedora
- Gentoo
- Debian
- Ubuntu
- Yellow Dog
- Suse
- Slackware
- Yoper
- Mandrakelinux
- Red Hat

Opacity

http://likethought.com/opacity/

(Mac OS X only)

Opacity is a powerful vector and bitmap editor designed particularly for creating screen graphics and resolution independent images. Its greatest strengths lie in what it calls variables and factories, and its resolution system. Variables and factories allow artwork to be exported automatically in a wide variety of formats and variations, while the resolution system makes it easy to create resolution-independent artwork. Rather than create several separate artworks for each size, Opacity can generate these for you, while also letting you control elements such as hiding details on smaller icons. This is particularly useful for creating icons and interface elements for iOS apps.

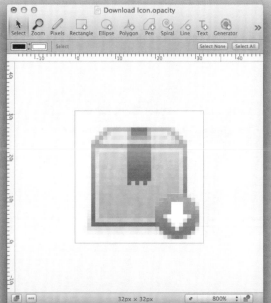

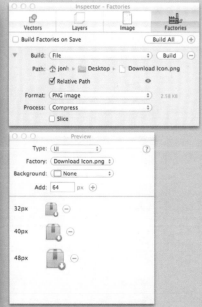

Sketch and Drawit

http://www.bohemiancoding.com/sketch

http://www.bohemiancoding.com/drawit

(Mac OS X only)

Sketch takes a different view to vector graphics from the outset. You start with an infinite canvas rather than specify a particular document size. You then use slices to export sections of the infinite canvas. Only since version 1.2 has it supported a pixel preview, suddenly making it very suitable for creating icons for screen as well as print.

Made by the same developer, Drawit is focused on non-destructive bitmap effects, but shares many of Sketch's vector tools. It also allows you to export to ICNS, but doesn't have any facility for setting up the various resources — only one resource can be saved to the file.

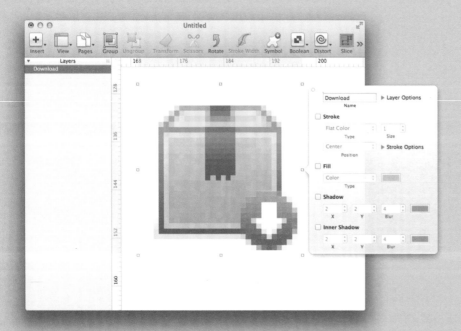

Cinema 4D and Maya

http://www.maxon.net/
http://usa.autodesk.com/maya/
(Windows and Mac OS X)

For those designers that prefer to create 3-D renders before applying touches in a program such as Photoshop, these are the leading choices.

Icon Composer

(Mac OS X only)

A simple utility provided as part of Mac or iOS Developer Tools for packaging separate images as either an ICO or an ICNS file. It is not as powerful as IconBuilder (for instance, it doesn't allow you to add different bit depths) but simple and straightforward to use.

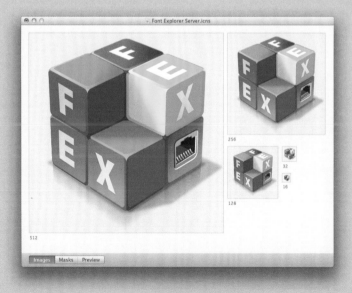

OmniGraffle

http://www.omnigroup.com/products/omnigraffle/
(Mac OS X only)

While not sold as a graphics editor, OmniGraffle does actually allow you to create vector artwork that can be exported as PNG and PDF (*http://steveweller.com/ articles/tabbar-icons/*).
It can be an option if you only need to create clean pictograms and you already have a copy.

X-Icon Editor

http://www.xiconeditor.com/

Microsoft's canvas-based online application for creating icons, specifically intended for creating favicons. It has the ability to include 16, 24, 32 and 64px resolutions and is free to use, so is handy if you're of a Yorkshire persuasion.

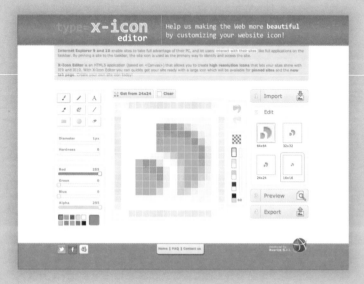

LiquidIcon XP

http://www.x2studios.com/OSX_Win_Products.html

(Windows only)

This is the free application I used for my icon workshop at our local primary school, as it was ideal for that purpose. It's a clear, lightweight, simple editor especially suited for making favicons as it only creates aliased artwork. It does the job!

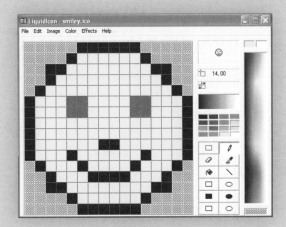

Pixen

https://github.com/philippec/Pixen

(Mac OS X only)

This application is limited to doing one thing well and that is pixel artwork. While you do get tools for creating shapes, there's no anti-aliasing here, perfect for unleashing your inner eboy (*http://hello.eboy.com/eboy/*). At the time of writing, there are no binaries available so you need to be comfortable building from source code!

Icon utilities

Candy Bar
http://www.omnigroup.com/products/omnigraffle/
(Mac OS X only)

CandyBar is not an app for creating icons, but rather a way of storing, organising, displaying and applying them to your Dock and application icons. Think of it as iPhoto for your icon collection, as well as a source of inspiration and ideas. It also has the ability to export icons and image files in a variety of bitmap formats, including ICNS and ICO.

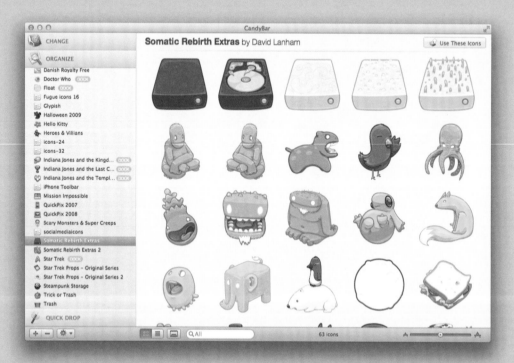

Preview
(Mac OS X only)

The easiest and default way to view the contents of ICNS or ICO files on Mac OS X. You can even drag the different size resources from the the sidebar to the Finder to export a particular size.

Icon reference chart

Throughout this book I've repeated the mantra 'it depends on the context' many times, as it really does change the approach and requirements of the icon. Well, here are those contexts! There is an accompanying online version available at *http://iconhandbook.co.uk/*, which is worth checking for updates and additions, as guidelines and OS requirements will change over time.

Conventions

There are two conventions used throughout this reference:

Sizing: All icons are square unless specified. For example, 32px is the same as 32 pixels × 32 pixels, but non-square icons would be referred to as 32 × 24px (32 pixels × 24 pixels). The size given in the first column is the canvas size: the physical size the icon file must be.

Safe area: This refers to a specified area that the icon must not overlap within the canvas size. For example, an icon may have a canvas size of 40px, but the safe area is 32px (4px padding). Some platforms refer to this as the focal area or safe frame, but not all specify a safe area.

All platforms

Sizes (px)	Format and naming	Notes
FAVICONS		
16px 32px 48px	favicon.ico .png .jpg .gif	While it can be useful to support multiple sizes other than 16px, these are optional. See chapter 3 for more detail on favicons.
OPERA BROWSER SPEED DIAL *Guidelines: http://dev.opera.com/articles/view/opera-speed-dial-enhancements/*		
Minimum: 114×114px Maximum: 256×160px	.png .jpg .gif	Shown when saving a site to Speed Dial, or in Speed Dial Extensions. Note that the viewed size depends on the zoom level, so don't aim for pixel perfection. Opera also supports apple-touch-icon.png and apple-touch-icon-precomposed.png where available.

::: BlackBerry.

Sizes (px)	Format and naming	Notes
APPLICATION ICONS *Smartphone Guidelines: http://docs.blackberry.com/en/developers/deliverables/28627/Dimensions_for_application_icons_1491552_11.jsp* *Playbook Guidelines: http://docs.blackberry.com/en/developers/deliverables/27299/Designing_application_icons_tablet_1401556_11.jsp*		
68px (Curve) 86px (PlayBook Tablet) 92px (Bold and Torch)	16-bit .png (Curve) 24-bit .png (Bold and Torch)	These icons should use a face-on perspective.
INDICATOR ICONS		
19px (Curve) 25px (Bold, Torch and PlayBook Tablet)	16-bit .png (Curve) 24-bit .png (Bold, Torch and PlayBook Tablet)	These are the flat, monochrome icons that appear in the banner, title bar, or in applications (indicators in a message list). Allow 2px padding top, left and right.

Google Android

Guidelines: *http://developer.android.com/guide/practices/ui_guidelines/icon_design.html*

Android icons require four separate sizes for different screen pixel densities:
Low: 120 dpi (ldpi)
Medium: 160dpi (mdpi)
High: 240 dpi (hdpi)
Extra high: 320dpi (xhdpi)

Also, be aware that the style changes occur fairly regularly with each major release, so it's always worth checking current guidelines!

Sizes (px)	Format and naming	Notes
LAUNCHER ICONS *Guidelines:* *http://developer.android.com/guide/practices/ui_guidelines/ icon_design_launcher.html*		
36px (ldpi) 48px (mdpi) 72px (hdpi) 96px (xhdpi) 512px (for the Android Market)	.png	Android encourages these to have unique outlines and include 4px padding.
ACTION BAR ICONS (ANDROID 3+) *Guidelines:* *http://developer.android.com/guide/practices/ui_guidelines/ icon_design_menu.html*		
18px (ldpi), 24px (mdpi), 36px (hdpi), 48px (xhdpi)	.png	These icons are used in the action bar menu. They should be face-on perspective and in greyscale.
STATUS BAR ICONS (ANDROID 3+) *Guidelines:* *http://developer.android.com/guide/practices/ui_guidelines/ icon_design_status_bar.html*		
18px (ldpi), 24px (mdpi), 36px (hdpi), 48px (xhdpi)	.png	These are used to represent application notifications in the status bar. They should be flat (no gradients), white and face-on perspective

Sizes (px)	Format and naming	Notes
TAB ICONS *Guidelines: http://developer.android.com/guide/practices/ui_guidelines/ icon_design_tab.html*		
24px (ldpi) 32px (mdpi) 48px (hdpi)	.png	These are used to represent individual tabs in a multi-tab interface. Each tab icon has two states: unselected and selected.
DIALOG AND LIST VIEW ICONS *Guidelines: http://developer.android.com/guide/practices/ui_guidelines/ icon_design_dialog.html* *http://developer.android.com/guide/practices/ui_guidelines/icon_design_list.html*		
24px (ldpi) 32px (mdpi) 48px (hdpi)	.png	These are shown in pop-up dialog boxes that prompt the user for interaction. They use a light gradient and inner shadow in order to stand out against a dark background. Unlike status bar icons, these use a specific gradient and inner shadow (see link above). List view icons are very similar, but they use an inner shadow effect showing the light source from above.

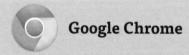 **Google Chrome**

Sizes (px)	Format and naming	Notes
CHROME EXTENSION ICON		
Guidelines: http://code.google.com/chrome/extensions/manifest.html		
16px 48px 128px	icon16.png icon48.png icon128.png	The 128px icon is the most important as this is used in the Chrome Web Store. The 48px is shown in the extensions list tab, while the 16px is used on infobars (*http://code.google.com/chrome/ extensions/experimental.infobars.html*).
CHROME WEB STORE APP ICON		
Guidelines: http://code.google.com/chrome/webstore/docs/images.html#icons		
128px	icon128.png	Perspective should be face-on and allow 16px padding.
GOOGLETV FAVICON		
Guidelines: http://code.google.com/tv/web/docs/design_for_tv.html		
96px	favicon.png	Link to it in the `<head>` of your HTML as you would for a normal favicon: `<link rel="icon" href="/favicon.png" type="image/png" />`

Guidelines: http://developer.apple.com/iphone/library/documentation/userexperience/ conceptual/mobilehig/IconsImages/IconsImages.html

Devices such as the iPhone 4 and 4S use a high resolution Retina display with twice the pixel density of other devices. Sizes can also vary for the iPad, and these are both indicated where applicable.

Sizes (px)	Format and naming	Notes
APPLICATION ICONS		
57px / 10px corner radius 114px / 20px corner radius (iPhone 4+) 72px / 12px corner radius (iPad)	.png Name icon for Retina display with a suffix of @2x.png	Do not include the corner radius in the artwork, and be aware that this portion is cropped.
WEB CLIP ICONS		
57px / 10px corner radius 114px / 20px corner radius (iPhone 4+) 72px / 12px corner radius (iPad)	apple-touch-icon-precomposed.png apple-touch-icon-114x114-precomposed.png (iPhone 4+) apple-touch-icon-72x72-precomposed.png	These are shown on the home screen when saving a bookmark. Leave off the '-precomposed' portion of the filename if you want iOS to add the glossy overlay. See chapter 3 for more information.
DOCUMENT ICONS		
22×29px 44×58px (iPhone 4+) 64px (iPad)	.png	These icons are overlaid on top of the standard document icon (white sheet of paper), hence the odd sizes. The iPad has a safe area of 44×59px.

iOS continued...

Sizes (px)	Format and naming	Notes
SPOTLIGHT/SETTINGS ICON		
29px / 5px corner radius 50px / 10px corner radius (iPhone 4+)	.png	iPad sizes are the same as for non-Retina displays, although the final visual size of this icon is 48×48px as iOS trims 1px from each side of the artwork and adds a drop shadow.
TOOLBAR AND NAVIGATION BAR ICONS		
20px 40px (iPhone 4+)	.png	iOS will use the alpha channel, applying shadow effects for you, so don't include any shadow in your artwork.
TAB BAR ICON		
30px 60px (iPhone 4+)	.png	
APP STORE ICON		
512px / 90px corner radius	Must be named 'iTunesArtwork' without the .png extension	The App Store icon is reduced to 176px square for the app's listing. iPad will use a scaled version of this icon for custom document icon, if one hasn't been provided.

Ubuntu

Guidelines: *http://tango.freedesktop.org/Tango_Icon_Theme_Guidelines*

Sizes (px)	Format and naming	Notes
APPLICATION AND DOCUMENT ICONS		
16px 22px 24px 32px 48px 64px 128px 256px	Separate .svg files for each resource	There isn't much documentation available for Linux online.

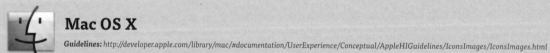

Mac OS X

Guidelines: http://developer.apple.com/library/mac/#documentation/UserExperience/Conceptual/AppleHIGuidelines/IconsImages/IconsImages.html

Sizes (px)	Format and naming	Notes
APPLICATION AND DOCUMENT ICONS		
16px 32px 128px 256px (OS X 10.5+) 512px (OS X 10.5+) 1,024px (OS X 10.7+)	applicationname.icns	Examples of how the icon resources are used: 16px - list views, spotlight searches 32px - Finder 128px - Dock, Finder previews 256px - Finder preview 512px - CoverFlow See chapter 7 for more information.
MENU BAR ICON		
Max 22px height×any width	.png,.tiff or .pdf	The convention is for greyscale only — use colour sparingly for attention/notification states.
SIDEBAR ICON		
16px (small) 18px (medium) 32px (large)	.pdf	From OS X 10.7+ the convention is for greyscale icons, with face-on perspective. The OS will ignore any colour you add and only use the alpha values.
TOOLBAR ICON (BUTTONS)		
32px (default) 24px (small size)	.icns, .pdf, multipage .tiff or .png	The small size is shown when the option is chosen via Customize Toolbar.
TOOLBAR ICON (STREAMLINED)		
19px	.pdf	These are used in monochrome toolbars where the icon is centred within a button (such as Mail and Safari). These have only one size.
SAFARI EXTENSION ICON		
16px (for the toolbar) 32px 48px	Icon-32.png Icon-48.png	Extensions are only supported in Safari 5+. The 16px icon is only required if the extension adds a button to the toolbar.

MeeGo

Guidelines: *http://www.developer.nokia.com/Resources/Library/Design_and_UX/designing-for-nokia-platforms/designing-for-meego-12-harmattan/meego-12-harmattan-iconography-guidelines.html*

The MeeGo and Symbian platforms used by Nokia are very similar, with minor canvas size and style differences.

Sizes (px)	Format and naming	Notes
LAUNCHER ICONS		
80px	.png	
LIST ICONS		
64px	.png	The pictogram should be contained within a 40px safe area, ideally 32px.
TOOLBAR ICONS		
40px	.png	

Guidelines: *http://www.developer.nokia.com/Resources/Library/Design_and_UX/designing-for-nokia-platforms/designing-for-symbian/symbian-iconography-guidelines.html*

Sizes (px)	Format and naming	Notes
LAUNCHER ICONS		
96px	.svgt (SVG Tiny)	Launcher icons have a 54px safe area for the main symbol to occupy.
LIST ICONS		
67×57px	.svgt (SVG Tiny)	List icons have a 47px safe area for the symbol to occupy.

Windows

Guidelines: http://msdn.microsoft.com/en-us/library/windows/desktop/aa511280.aspx

Sizes (px)	Format and naming	Notes
APPLICATION, DOCUMENT AND CONTROL PANEL ICONS		
16px 24px* 32px 48px 64px* 128px 256px (Windows Vista+) * Required for classic mode	.ico	Microsoft recommends including 8-bit and 4-bit images for each resource. The style of XP icons is more saturated in Vista onwards. See chapter 7 for more information.
TOOLBAR ICONS		
16px 24px 32px	.ico, .png	These should always be face-on perspective, even at 32px.
DIALOG AND WIZARD ICONS		
32px 48px	.ico, .png	
QUICK LAUNCH AREA		
40px 48px	.ico, .png	As the 48px resource will be scaled down for the Alt+Tab overlay, it's recommended to add a 40px resource for crispness.
BALLOON ICONS		
32px 40px	.ico, .png	

Windows Phone 7 (Metro)

Guidelines: http://msdn.microsoft.com/en-us/library/hh202915(v=VS.92).aspx

The Windows Phone style is very consistent — both application and toolbar icons are focused on strong monochrome pictograms that contrast well with a background colour.

Sizes (px)	Format and naming	Notes
APPLICATION ICONS		
62px (Applications list) 99px (Windows Phone Marketplace - small) 173px (Tile image and Windows Marketplace) 200px (Desktop application icon for Windows Marketplace)	.png	Start tiles are a key part of the Windows Phone UI. As well as the icon, the tile will contain other information from the application such as number of unread emails.
APPLICATION BAR ICONS *Guidelines:* http://msdn.microsoft.com/en-us/library/ff431806(v=vs.92).aspx		
48px	.png	These icons should be rendered in white only and be kept within a safe area of 26px. Don't include the circle bordering the icon as this is provided by the OS, which will also recolour it to work when the light theme is enabled.

Index

A

Q

R

S

W

wallet icon **134**
Walsh, Cian **252**
warning signs **4, 37, 42, 112**
wastebasket symbol **15**
Web Semantics **194, 211**
webkit browsers **79, 184, 199, 203**
 see also Google Chrome; Safari
website display **187–97**
white transparency **144**
Widmann, Johannes **3**
Williams, Josh **51–3**
Wilson, Drew **197**
Windows icons:
 application icons **216, 221**
 history **22, 278**
 icon reference **303–4**
 viewing angle **216, 263**
Windows 7:
 icons **67, 221, 262**
 pinned site **63**
 taskbar **80**
Windows Aero glass **62, 273**
Windows display preferences **155**
Windows Phone 7 **304**
Windows toolbar image strips **120**
Windows Vista **221, 259, 261–4, 303**
Windows XP **215, 221, 262–3, 290, 303**
wireframes **94, 237**
Wooten, Adam **39**

X

X-Icon editor **289**
Xerox Star Workstation (Xerox 8010) **13, 14, 22**
XML (Extensible Markup Language) *see* SVG
xScope icon **177**

Y

Yoshida, Kenichi **237, 253, 278**

Z

Zilmer, Priidu **45–6**
zooming **176, 187, 190, 208–9, 294**